Supporting Children with Speech and Language Difficulties

Completely revised and updated in light of the new 2014 SEND Code of Practice, this new edition describes the different types of difficulties experienced by pupils with speech, language and communication needs. It will help teachers and other professionals feel more confident by providing expert guidance and practical strategies, and as a professional development tool, will also encourage outstanding practice by suggesting ideas and materials for in-house training sessions. The wide-ranging and accessible chapters explore topics including:

- Listening skills
- Phonological awareness
- Comprehension of language
- Activities for circle time
- Working with parents

Featuring useful checklists, templates and photocopiable resources, this practical text contains a wealth of valuable advice and tried-and-tested strategies for identifying children and young people with speech, language and communication needs, ensuring they have the support they need to make exceptional progress.

Cathy Allenby – Teacher in the Language Unit of the Adult, Children and Family Services, Hull City Council, UK

Judith Fearon-Wilson – Teacher in the Language Unit of the Adult, Children and Family Services, Hull City Council, UK

Sally Merrison – Specialist Speech and Language Therapist, UK

Elizabeth Morling – Series Editor, SEN Consultant and former Head of the Education Service for Physical Disability, Hull City Council, UK

nasen is a professional membership association that supports all those who work with or care for children and young people with special and additional educational needs. Members include teachers, teaching assistants, support workers, other educationalists, students and parents.

nasen supports its members through policy documents, journals, its magazine Special!, publications, professional development courses, regional networks and newsletters. Its website contains more current information such as responses to government consultations. nasen's published documents are held in very high regard both in the UK and internationally.

Other titles published in association with the National Association for Special Educational Needs (nasen):

Language for Learning in the Secondary School: A practical guide for supporting students with speech, language and communication needs
Sue Hayden and Emma Jordan
2012/pb: 978-0-415-61975-2

Using Playful Practice to Communicate with Special Children
Margaret Corke
2012/pb: 978-0-415-68767-6

The Equality Act for Educational Professionals: A simple guide to disability and inclusion in schools
Geraldine Hills
2012/pb: 978-0-415-68768-3

More Trouble with Maths: A teacher's complete guide to identifying and diagnosing mathematical difficulties
Steve Chinn
2012/pb: 978-0-415-67013-5

Dyslexia and Inclusion: Classroom Approaches for Assessment, Teaching and Learning, 2ed
Gavin Reid
2012/pb: 978-0-415-60758-2

Promoting and Delivering School-to-School Support for Special Educational Needs: A practical guide for SENCOs
Rita Cheminais
2013/pb 978-0-415-63370-3

Time to Talk: Implementing outstanding practice in speech, language and communication
Jean Gross
2013/pb: 978-0-415-63334-5

Curricula for Teaching Children and Young People with Severe or Profound and Multiple Learning Difficulties: Practical strategies for educational professionals
Peter Imray and Viv Hinchcliffe
2013/pb: 978-0-415-83847-4

Successfully Managing ADHD: A handbook for SENCOs and teachers
Fintan O'Regan
2014/pb: 978-0-415-59770-8

Brilliant Ideas for Using ICT in the Inclusive Classroom, 2ed
Sally McKeown and Angela McGlashon
2015/pb: 978-1-138-80902-4

Boosting Learning in the Primary Classroom: Occupational therapy strategies that really work with pupils
Sheilagh Blyth
2015/pb: 978-1-13-882678-6

Beating Bureaucracy in Special Educational Needs, 3ed
Jean Gross
2015/pb: 978-1-138-89171-5

Transforming Reading Skills in the Secondary School: Simple strategies for improving literacy
Pat Guy
2015/pb: 978-1-138-89272-9

Supporting Children with Speech and Language Difficulties, 2ed
Cathy Allenby, Judith Fearon-Wilson, Sally Merrison and Elizabeth Morling
2015/pb: 978-1-138-85511-3

Supporting Children with Dyspraxia and Motor Co-ordination Difficulties, 2ed
Susan Coulter, Lesley Kynman, Elizabeth Morling, Rob Grayson and Jill Wing
2015/pb: 978-1-138-85507-6

Developing Memory Skills in the Primary Classroom: A complete programme for all
Gill Davies
2015/pb: 978-1-138-89262-0

Language for Learning in the Primary School: A practical guide for supporting pupils with language and communication difficulties across the curriculum, 2ed
Sue Hayden and Emma Jordan
2015/pb: 978-1-138-89862-2

Supporting Children with Autistic Spectrum Disorders, 2ed
Elizabeth Morling and Colleen O'Connell
2016/pb: 978-1-138-85514-4

Understanding and Supporting Pupils with Moderate Learning Difficulties in the Secondary School: A practical guide
Rachael Hayes and Pippa Whittaker
2016/pb: 978-1-138-01910-2

Assessing Children with Specific Learning Difficulties: A teacher's practical guide
Gavin Reid, Gad Elbeheri and John Everatt
2016/pb: 978-0-415-67027-2

Supporting Children with Down's Syndrome, 2ed
Lisa Bentley, Ruth Dance, Elizabeth Morling, Susan Miller and Susan Wong
2016/pb: 978-1-138-91485-8

Provision Mapping and the SEND Code of Practice: Making it work in primary, secondary and special schools, 2ed
Anne Massey
2016/pb: 978-1-138-90707-2

Supporting Children with Medical Conditions, 2ed
Susan Coulter, Lesley Kynman, Elizabeth Morling, Francesca Murray, Jill Wing and Rob Grayson
2016/pb: 978-1-13-891491-9

Supporting Children with Speech and Language Difficulties

Second edition

Cathy Allenby, Judith Fearon-Wilson, Sally Merrison and Elizabeth Morling

Routledge
Taylor & Francis Group

LONDON AND NEW YORK

Helping Everyone Achieve ■■■

This edition published 2015
by Routledge
2 Park Square, Milton Park, Abingdon, Oxon OX14 4RN

and by Routledge
711 Third Avenue, New York, NY 10017

Routledge is an imprint of the Taylor & Francis Group, an informa business

First published 2004 by Hull Learning Services

British Library Cataloguing in Publication Data
A catalogue record for this book is available from the British Library

Library of Congress Cataloging-in-Publication Data
Allenby, Cathy.
Supporting children with speech and language difficulties / Cathy Allenby, Judith Fearon-Wilson, Sally Merrison and Liz Morling. -- 2nd edition.
pages cm
1. Language disorders in children. 2. Speech therapy for children. 3. Children with social disabilities--Education. I. Fearon-Wilson, Judith. II. Merrison, Sally. III. Morling, Liz. IV. Title.
RJ496.L35A47 2015
618.92'855--dc23
2014045448

ISBN: 978-1-138-85510-6 (hbk)
ISBN: 978-1-138-85511-3 (pbk)
ISBN: 978-1-315-72053-1 (ebk)

Typeset in Helvetica
by Fakenham Prepress Solutions, Fakenham, Norfolk NR21 8NN

Contents

Foreword

This book was written in partnership with Kingston Upon Hull Special Educational Needs Support Service (SENSS) and the Hull and East Riding Speech and Language Therapy Support Service.

It is one of a series of titles, providing an up-to-date overview of special educational needs for SENCOs, teachers and other professionals and parents. It was produced in response to the needs of a growing number of children requiring support with speech and language difficulties.

It was written and compiled by:

Cathy Allenby and Judith Fearon-Wilson
(Kingston Upon Hull SEN Support Service).

Thanks are given to the Hull and East Riding Speech and Language Therapy Support Service for their guidance when compiling this book.

Our thanks too to senior adviser John Hill for his support and encouragement throughout the development of this series.

It has now been updated to reflect current practice and legislation in education by:

Cathy Allenby (Specialist Teacher, Language Unit, Hull)
Judith Fearon-Wilson (Specialist Teacher, Language Unit, Hull)
Sally Merrison (Specialist Speech and Language Therapist)
Liz Morling (Series Editor).

1   Introduction

(Taken from 'I CAN', the national educational charity for children with speech and language difficulties.)

For most children, learning to communicate is something that happens naturally. However, for some children, something goes wrong. It's not always known why it happens, but it's more common than most people think. It has been estimated that over one million children in the UK have some kind of speech and language difficulty, which is equivalent to around one child in every classroom.

What is a speech, language or communication difficulty?

The term 'speech, language and/or communication difficulty' is an umbrella term, covering a wide range of speech, language and communication delays and disorders.

- Some children may have difficulty using certain sounds in words and can be unintelligible when they talk.
- Others have difficulty understanding words. Their vocabulary is small and they find gaining and remembering words extremely hard. These children need a lot of help extending their vocabulary, for example in school with subjects such as history and science, which have many specialist words.
- Some children have severe problems with grammar. For example, they might not be aware of the 'ed' marker at the end of a regular verb. As a result they would describe something that happened in the past as in the present tense.
- Others have difficulty coping with the order of words. A sentence such as 'the boy was pushed by the girl' may be interpreted as 'the girl was pushed by the boy'.
- Some children have none of the above difficulties. They can pronounce words clearly, learn and remember new words and are able to put them in the right order using the correct grammar. Their difficulty lies in understanding or using words which express abstract ideas. Concepts such as time and distance hold little or no meaning. Their language is at a very literal level and they often do not see hidden meanings or implications.
- Language difficulties can affect children's ability to read and write. For example, if children are not perceiving sounds accurately they won't be able to reproduce them in spoken or written form.
- We use language to form relationships with others. Some youngsters with language difficulties find building friendships very difficult.

This is only a selection of the language and communication difficulties that children may experience and many may be affected by more than one.

Speech difficulties are easy to spot. By contrast, language difficulties can be more difficult to pinpoint and diagnose. In fact the latter are often called the 'hidden' learning difficulty. It is vital that class teachers feel that they are able to identify difficulties and incorporate appropriate objectives and strategies into their planning and differentiation.

The aim of this book is to provide class teachers with suggestions that will help them feel more able to support these children in school.

2 Inclusion in education

In order to understand the issues of speech, language and communication difficulties within the framework of the inclusion agenda, the following statements should be taken into consideration:

The Special Education Needs and Disability Code of Practice (2014) states that special educational needs and provision can be considered as falling under four broad areas:

1. Communication and interaction
2. Cognition and learning
3. Social, mental and emotional health
4. Sensory and/or physical.

Many children and young people have difficulties that fit clearly into one of these areas; some have needs that span two or more areas; for others the precise nature of their need may not be clear at the outset. It is therefore important to carry out a detailed individual assessment of each child or young person and their situation at the earliest opportunity to make an accurate assessment of their needs.

Communication and interaction

Children and young people with SEN may have difficulties in one or more of the areas of speech, language and communication. These children and young people need help to develop their linguistic competence in order to support their thinking, as well as their communication skills. Specific learning difficulties such as dyslexia or a physical or sensory impairment such as hearing loss may also lead to communication difficulties.

Those with speech, language and communication needs (SLCN) cover the whole ability range. They find it more difficult to communicate with others. They may have problems taking part in conversations, either because they find it difficult to understand what others say or because they have difficulties with fluency and forming sounds, words and sentences. It may be that when they hear or see a word they are not able to understand its meaning, leading to words being used incorrectly or out of context and the child having a smaller vocabulary. It may be a combination of these problems. For some children and young people, difficulties may become increasingly apparent as the language they need to understand and use becomes more complex.

Provision for children and young people with communication and interaction difficulties should reflect their likely need for support in developing social relationships and their increased risk of emotional or mental health problems. It may also cover support in making progress in related areas of learning such as literacy. Interventions might include creating rich oral language environments, individual support and augmentative and alternative means of communication.

In order to understand the issues of **speech**, **language** and **communication** difficulties within the framework of the inclusion agenda, the following statements should be taken into consideration:

- Inclusion recognises that all children have different abilities and experiences and seeks to value and gain from these differences. It is not about expecting or trying to make everyone the same or behave in the same way.
- Inclusion in education involves the process of increasing the participation of students in, and reducing their exclusion from, the cultures, curricula and communities of local schools.
- Inclusion involves restructuring the cultures, policies and practices in schools so that they respond to the diversity of students in their locality.
- Inclusion is concerned with the learning and participation of all students vulnerable to exclusionary pressures, not only those with impairments or those who are categorised as having 'special educational needs'.
- Inclusion is concerned with improving schools for staff as well as for students.
- A concern with overcoming barriers to the access and participation of particular students may reveal gaps in the attempts of a school to respond to diversity more generally.
- All students have a right to an education in their locality.
- Diversity is not viewed as a problem to overcome, but as a rich resource to support the learning of all.
- Inclusion is concerned with fostering mutually sustaining relationships between schools and communities.
- Inclusion in education is one aspect of inclusion in society.

An inclusive culture is one in which:

- Everyone is made to feel welcome.
- Students help each other.
- Staff collaborate with each other.
- Staff and students treat one another with respect.
- There is a partnership between staff and parents/carers.
- All local communities are involved with the school.
- Staff and governors work well together.

Inclusive values are established when:

- There are high expectations of all students.
- Everyone has a philosophy of inclusion.
- Students are equally valued.
- Staff seek to remove all barriers to learning and participation in school.
- The school strives to minimise discriminatory practices.

4

3 Flowchart: how can I help?

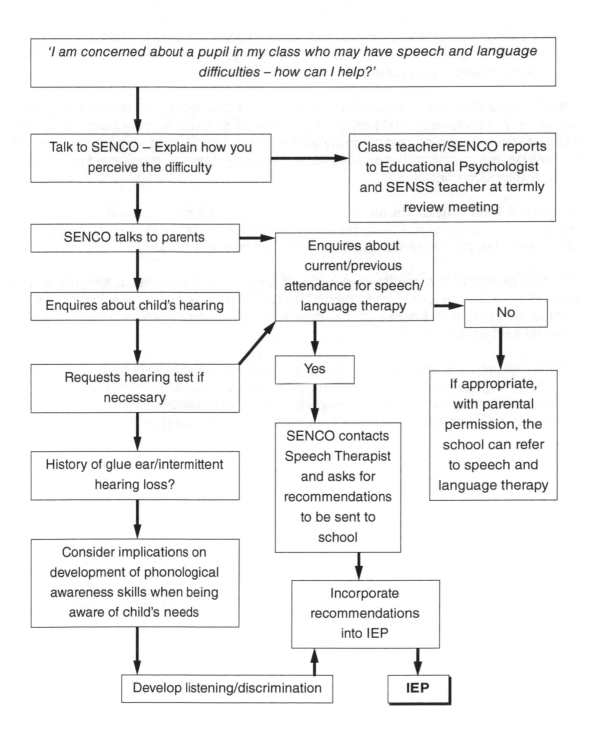

'*I am concerned about a pupil in my class who may have speech and language difficulties – how can I help?*'

Talk to SENCO – Explain how you perceive the difficulty

Class teacher/SENCO reports to Educational Psychologist and SENSS teacher at termly review meeting

SENCO talks to parents

Enquires about current/previous attendance for speech/ language therapy

No

Enquires about child's hearing

Requests hearing test if necessary

Yes

If appropriate, with parental permission, the school can refer to speech and language therapy

History of glue ear/intermittent hearing loss?

SENCO contacts Speech Therapist and asks for recommendations to be sent to school

Consider implications on development of phonological awareness skills when being aware of child's needs

Incorporate recommendations into IEP

Develop listening/discrimination

IEP

4   Attention, listening and memory skills

The following pages look at the areas of attention control, listening skills, memory and phonological awareness, which, while not language skills in themselves, are all vital precursors to language and learning.

Attention control refers to the ability to focus on a task and switch attention between activities. A school-age child would be expected to listen to information from the teacher while engaging in an activity at the same time. A child who is unable to do this will be at a considerable disadvantage. Language learning requires a fairly mature level of attention control.

Similarly if **listening skills** are poor, the child will find it difficult to learn new vocabulary and to acquire more sophisticated language skills. S/he may have difficulty developing the phonic skills necessary to be an effective reader.

The role of short-term **auditory memory** is also of great importance for it allows the child to hold and process information. The child who has memory difficulties will be unable to respond to follow instructions within the classroom and may well go on to have difficulties with reading.

Phonological awareness is the ability to recognise sounds within words. This may include recognising and discriminating between sounds within words, hearing and providing rhyming words or breaking up words into syllables. All these skills are important in the development of both spoken and written language.

5 Attention control: developmental stages

(From *Helping Language Development* by Cooper, Moodley and Reynell.)

Age levels are approximate; there is great variability.

Stage 1   During first year of life
Extreme distractibility – child's attention held momentarily by whatever is the dominant stimulus.

Stage 2   Second year
Inflexible and rigid attention – child can concentrate for some time on a task of his own choice, but cannot tolerate any adult intervention. Attention level is best where the activity is one of his own choosing.

Stage 3   Third year
Single-channelled attention, but becoming more flexible. With adult's help can focus attention. Child can transfer from his task to adult's direction, and back to task. Attention is still adult-directed making it necessary for the teacher to ensure s/he has the child's attention before giving instructions.

Stage 4   Fourth year
Still single-channelled to one task, but child can now transfer it spontaneously. Moves gradually to the stage where s/he only needs to look at the speaker if directions are difficult to understand.

Stage 5
Two-channelled attention, where the child is now able to attend to verbal instructions in relation to the task without actually looking at the adult. Attention can only be sustained for short periods of time.

Stage 6
Mature school entry level, where integrated attention is well established and well sustained.

N.B. You may see fluctuating levels depending on environment or task complexity.

6 General activities and strategies to develop attention and listening skills

- Work with the child in a quiet, distraction-free environment, thus allowing the child to focus on the activity presented.
- Gradually start to work with the child in their normal environment as this allows him/her gradually to accommodate the distractions normally present and begin to focus on the activity.
- Ensure that the activities are both interesting and developmentally appropriate for the child.
- To engage the child's interest, always address him/her by name and when s/he has responded, encourage eye contact with the speaker.
- Try to establish shared attention to a common point of reference where possible.
- Encourage the child to follow your line of gaze or notice as you point to things, for example, looking at books and exploring objects and activities together will encourage a common shared interest.
- Accompany verbal requests to 'look' by clearly pointing to the item.
- Make the most of any opportunity to give the child guidance in order to proceed with, or complete, an activity. Do not always allow a free hand to complete tasks. Instead you can build in adult direction, for example, by spreading out the pieces of a jigsaw puzzle and indicating, by pointing to the piece you want them to select, and saying, 'where does this piece go?'
- Be sure to give praise when the child responds appropriately.
- Use simple construction or pull-apart toys to demonstrate, 'which piece goes where?'
- Choose activities which are easy to complete so that your guidance is needed. Use language models such as, 'look, it goes here' or 'this piece now'.
- The child will benefit from 'copy cat' games, where they have to copy actions modelled by the adult. Encourage them to copy your actions, which should always be accompanied by spoken instructions, for example, 'clap your hands, tap your feet', etc.
- Encourage the child to join in with finger rhymes and action rhymes.
- Note when the child is more likely to use eye contact spontaneously. Reinforce this by repeating these activities whenever possible.
- Keep language clear and simple. Try to ensure that the child gives you his full attention by saying, 'Peter, look at me and listen.'
- The child will need to play games that develop turn-taking skills. Interactive stories and lift-the-flap books can be used where the child will take turns to lift the flaps, etc. Taking turns to play a musical instrument will also help to develop turn-taking skills.

For many children, these activities begin on a 1:1 basis before moving to a small group setting. It is important that when working in a small group you consider the attention levels of the other children so that you can differentiate the activity appropriately.

7   Specific strategies to develop Attention Levels 1–5

Level 1

Aim: To attract and sustain the child's attention to people, objects and events in his/her environment.

- Encourage good eye contact by drawing attention to your eyes and saying 'Can you look at my eyes?' – anything to get the child looking at your face.
- Use the child's name frequently, but make it purposeful.
- Visual prompts and signs can also be used to sustain attention and understanding.

Level 2

Aim: To help the child tolerate the adult's presence and involvement in an activity.

- First sit with him/her and watch.
- Then sit beside him/her and engage in parallel play.
- When the child can tolerate the adult and begins to imitate the adult, small modifications can be made to his/her own play, e.g. pass a jigsaw piece to him/her or add a brick.
- Gradually accompany actions with integral verbal instructions, e.g. 'The brick goes on top.'

Level 3

Aim: To establish the child's own control over his/her focus of attention. Some of these activities are suitable for a small group.

- Present the child with task materials and allow a few minutes for exploratory play. Before giving any verbal directions make sure that s/he is sitting still and is not fiddling with the toys then call his/her name, establish eye contact and deliver a short simple instruction, e.g. ask the child to copy shapes onto paper.
- The next step is to gain the child's attention while s/he is actively engaged in the task. Call his/her name, say 'look', 'listen', but do not give an instruction until you have established eye contact.
- Gradually decrease the number of alerting activities needed, until the child can look up and listen when just his/her name is called.

Level 4

Aim: To begin to transfer attention skills to the group or classroom. Slowly teach the child to listen and take in what you say without stopping what s/he is doing, by following these steps:

- Alert the child to your presence while s/he is performing a task, e.g. jigsaw, by calling his/her name and giving a brief clear instruction.
- Stand by the child without speaking until s/he is aware of you, and then give the instruction.
- If the child looks up at you encourage him/her to continue with the task with comments such as 'don't look up, that's very good.'
- Stand behind the child occasionally, while commenting on his/her activity. S/he cannot therefore look at you without turning right around.

Level 5

Aim: To increase the child's concentration span and continue to transfer to the classroom situation.

- The child should now be able to work alongside another child doing the same activity.
- Increase his/her tolerance by including him/her in a small group of children with a similar attention level.

8 Processing information in the classroom

(Based on Ellis and Young's model of reading.)

Weaknesses at any stage can affect the later processes. Strengths can be used to support weaker processes.

Auditory processing

- Identifies individual sounds from speech.
- Copes with background noise and mispronunciations.
- Poor skills affect the development of the semantic system.

Visual processing

- Important features are recognised and matched to a store of known words.

The semantic system

- A store for word meanings and associations.
- Word-finding difficulties can be seen if the semantic fields are weak, e.g. lion/tiger, plum/pear.
- The system may be weak because of poor auditory processing but can also support auditory discrimination difficulties.

Letter-sound conversion

- Letters are converted into speech sounds.

Assembly

- The spoken word is stored and accessed here.
- There can be errors such as 'par cark'.
- Words do not have to be spoken aloud. They can be read using the 'inner voice'.

9 How does a child process language?

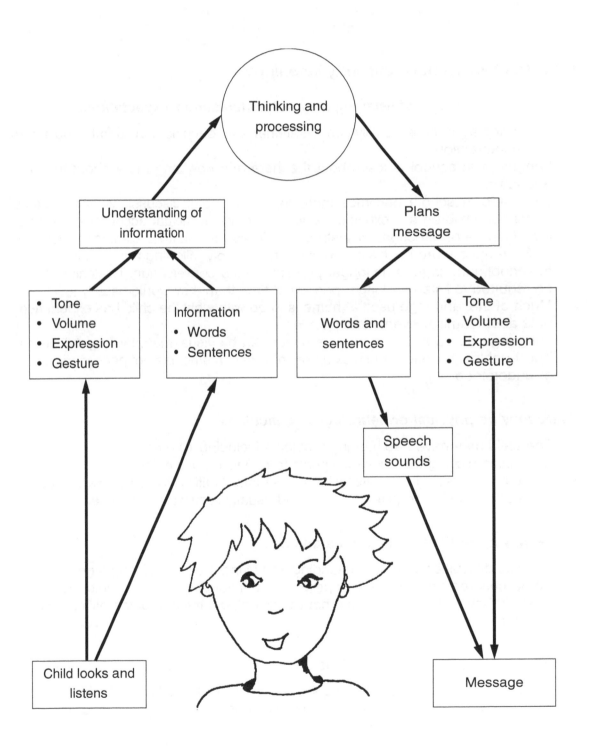

10 Listening skills

Why do children have difficulty listening?

Previous experiences of listening may not match school expectations

- Language at home is usually conversational, with each person contributing in turn to the interaction.
- Language at school is less about the 'here and now' and more about the 'past and future'.
- Language in school becomes more formalised, e.g, discussions and debates. In school, children are expected to follow stories or factual accounts or perhaps make sense of directions or instructions. These are familiar classroom activities which require more sophisticated skills than simply following a conversation.
- In school, language is no longer presented as a conversation. The children may be required to listen for longer periods of time than they would usually.
- Much of the language used at home is to do with what the child has experienced or is about familiar events and people.
- Language heard at home may be supported by visual material (e.g. television). This enables the listener to pick up on information s/he has not necessarily heard or understood.

There may be physical or neurological difficulties

- The child may have had hearing problems including 'glue ear'.
- Difficulties picking out relevant signals from background noise.
- Auditory processing difficulties which may make it difficult to perceive and produce.
- Extended listening requires practice and usually requires a response.

There may be difficulties in understanding

- Specific difficulties with understanding and using the rules of language.
- Some children are unable to cope with understanding too much information. As a result they may switch off and not listen well, but the root of the difficulty lies in understanding.

There may be motivation difficulties

- Anxiety and stress may make a child withdrawn and unable to participate.
- ADHD – Attention Deficit Hyperactivity Disorder.

- Children can either be ready and eager to listen or they may be switched off and unwilling to listen for other reasons.

Promoting listening skills required for the school environment

Pupils need to learn how to become active thinkers in school situations and to cope with more complex language such as prediction and hypothesis.

As mentioned above, many young children experience difficulties trying to keep up with the pace of learning currently required in Literacy. It is vital therefore that they are taught the skills required for good listening and are able to think clearly and formulate their own ideas.

Helping children with listening difficulties

- Check the child's hearing.
- Check whether the child understands.
- Practise 'active listening' (see below).
- Practise listening in simple games and activities (see suggestions).
- Monitor listening skills throughout activities.
- Discuss the consequences of correct and incorrect behaviours within an activity.
- Encourage evaluation of others' listening skills.
- Encourage evaluation of child's own listening skills.

Teaching 'active listening'

Some children need to learn about listening by talking about it and practising it in simple activities.

What does listening involve?

Identify the associated behaviours to do with listening:

- Looking at the person.
- Concentrating on a shared topic.
- Being still.

'Active listening' involves the use of simple strategies that encourage the listener to participate actively in the learning environment. This may involve asking for clarification if understanding breaks down.

The child will need to be taught the rules for 'good listening' and to be helped to recognise these behaviours in him/herself and others. Role play will be useful to demonstrate '**good** listening' and '**not good** listening'. This can be carried out in a group situation.

The rules are:

- Sitting still.
- Looking at the speaker.
- Thinking about the words.

See the 'Good listening rules' chart in the Appendix.

So, while the teacher speaks, another adult could deliberately fidget, stare out of the window, or answer incorrectly, so that the children can call out 'not sitting still!' or 'not looking!' or 'not thinking!' as appropriate. When the children recognise these behaviours in others it will be possible to tell them in a completely neutral voice that they are not doing 'good sitting', etc.

Pupils need to realise that they have to be ready to listen. Attention to how they sit and where they look is one of the first steps and precedes the thinking part of the activity. Once the children appear focused they need to take part in a range of activities that promote thinking skills.

It is also important to praise the behaviour of the children in the group and give them clear feedback. This will provide good role models for the child.

It is important to be interactive with the child to make learning happen.

Transfer to classroom – we cannot expect children to do it immediately in the classroom. Encourage transfer of skills gradually.

Introduce activities which require a response:

✔ Oral comprehension tasks.
✔ Auditory odd-one-out activities.
✔ Word association games.
✔ Following instructions.

Monitor the responses

- If someone cannot provide an appropriate response, come back to them on another occasion. Some children think that once they have had their turn they can sit back passively.
- Analyse incorrect responses and try to work out why the child made the error, e.g. was s/he not listening or was some part of the question or subject matter not understood?
- Are there particular types of activity which are proving difficult? Consider why this may be so.

11 Activities to improve listening ability

- **Read the child a story** – ask him/her to signal to you whenever s/he hears a particular word, e.g. an animal noise or a child's name.
- **Listen to different sounds/noises** – ask the child to signal only when s/he hears a particular sound.
- **Sequence different sounds in the correct order** – ask the child to identify various sounds and then make two sounds and ask him/her to recall the order in which they were made. Then try three, four sounds.
- **Ask the child to listen in a quiet environment** and then ask him/her to draw the things s/he hears.
- **Listen for your sound game** – make up a story that requires each child in the group to respond with a sound every time the child hears the name of the object/ animal, e.g. doorbell, telephone, radio, cat. As the story will be made up by the teacher/adult the responses from the pupils can direct the listening responses required.
- **Where is the sound coming from?** – ask the child to stand in the centre of a circle with his/her eyes closed. Somebody from the circle makes a noise, e.g. clapping, and the child has to identify where the sound is coming from.
- **Hide a clockwork toy** somewhere in the room. Ask the child to find it by listening. Gradually make the sounds quieter.
- **Listen for loud and soft sounds** – use a variety of items to help the child discriminate the differences.
- **Make up silly sentences** – look at a picture together and make some deliberate, silly mistakes when talking about it. Encourage the child to tell you what is wrong.
- **Instructional activities** – colouring/drawing pictures from precise details, e.g. draw a house shape, put four windows on it, draw a tree, put apples on it, etc. Make it into a game by using an 'alarm', e.g. a shaker or drum. If the child does something wrong sound the 'alarm'. Each time the alarm goes off s/he loses a life.
- **'Simon Says', 'Musical Statues'** – a variation on Musical Statues is when the music stops, ask the pupils to do something, e.g. clap hands, touch nose, sit down.

All games need to be cognitively simple. This is important to keep the emphasis on developing listening.

12 Listening and auditory memory

Memory skills play an important part in understanding and using language effectively. A child's difficulties in following instructions may, to varying degrees, be due to problems of auditory short-term memory.

For example, if the class teacher says to a class, 'Finish the sentence you are on, put away your pencils, close your books and line up at the door', there are some children for whom this will represent a memory-overload. If these children also have difficulties with the syntax and grammar involved, then their difficulties will be compounded.

Strategies to aid auditory memory skills

Multi-sensory strategies

✔ **Touch** (holding an object or simply touching it)
✔ **Visualising** (looking at the object or picturing it in your mind)
✔ **Verbalising** (repeating what it is you wish to remember)

(These skills are hierarchical and as the child develops s/he will be able to call on each of these areas to a greater degree.)

✔ **Put spoken language into separate units of meaning.** Speak clearly and pause between each part of the instruction/explanation, e.g. 'Put your book in the tray/give your pencil to Peter/and read a book'.
✔ **Ask the child to repeat the message or instruction** to ensure that s/he has understood. This will check if the child has grasped the main points.
✔ **Use visual reminders** in the form of objects, pictures, simple drawings or symbols in a simple checklist (see visual memory recommendations).
✔ **Encourage the child to seek clarification.** If the child forgets encourage him/ her to ask for clarification. It is important that the adult models exactly what the child needs to say, e.g. 'Can't remember the last bit, can you say it again please?' etc. Praise other children in the class when they seek clarification so that it is seen as a sensible strategy when the child is unsure.
✔ **Barrier games** – the teacher and child sit with a screen between them. The teacher provides the child with a piece of paper and gives the child simple drawing/ colouring instructions. The teacher also draws/colours the precise instructions s/he gives the child. When the barrier is removed the child has instant feedback.

✔ **Sing songs and rhymes to build auditory memory.**
For example:
a) 'I went to the shop and I bought...' game. The first child says an item then the next child says the first item and another and so on.
b) 'I packed my case and I took...' game.
c) 'I went to the zoo and I saw...' game.

At a slightly higher level:
d) 'I went to the library and I read...'
e) 'I went to the cinema and I saw...'

✔ **Read stories in small groups.** Gradually lengthen them. Ask the pupils to recall in a simple sequence. (Simple repetitive stories that are interactive can be used at first.)
✔ **Use both taped stories and dramatised stories.**
✔ **Develop auditory sequencing by encouraging the pupils to select objects at a fast pace.**
✔ **Teach the child the language of sequencing: first, next, last, start, finish, etc.**
✔ **Use 'circle time' activities** (see recommendations on page 48). Pass an object around a circle and everybody makes a comment about it. No repetitions are allowed, e.g. 'It is yellow', 'It is for eating', 'It tastes sour', etc.

13 Phonological awareness

Phonological awareness and literacy development

Phonological awareness is the ability to perceive sounds within words.

It can also be defined as the development of sound skills that precedes literacy development.

Delayed development of phonological awareness skills can manifest itself initially in speech development difficulties and later in the development of early literacy skills.

Findings consistently confirm that of all the factors that can predict a child's later reading success (e.g. intelligence, being read to, language ability) the most powerful is the level of phonological awareness possessed by the child in the first year at school.

Research also tells us that phonological awareness can be taught and that to be most effective in literacy development, once the prerequisite sound skills have been taught, the programme should formally introduce the link between sounds and letters.

Phonological awareness skills include:	
• Rhyming	– of words ending with the same group of sounds
• Alliteration	– of beginning sounds
• Isolation	– of sounds within words, e.g. initial sounds
• Segmentation	– of sentences and words into component parts
• Blending	– of word parts and sounds into words
• Exchange	– of sounds to make new combinations, e.g. mat – pat

14 Teaching phonological awareness

Many phonological awareness training programmes have been developed and are available from various sources. While they differ in presentation and in the resources provided, there is an overall pattern in the stages of development and order of activities prescribed; they include:

Stage 1   Listening to sounds

Rhyming   –   recognition, matching, odd-one-out activities
Alliteration   –   beginning sounds

Stage 2   Awareness of rhyme

Rhyming   –   creation of rhyme
                          e.g. *Which one sounds the same as.........?*
                          Tell me a word that rhymes with.........?
Alliteration   –   beginning sounds
                          e.g. *Which one starts the same as.........?*
Isolation   –   beginning and ending sounds
                          e.g. *What is the last sound you hear in.........?*
Segmentation –   syllables, 2 and 3 phoneme words
                          e.g. *How many beats/syllables can you hear in.........?*

Stage 3   Using skills to manipulate other sounds/words

Segmentation –   identification of sounds/phonemes in 3 and 4 letter words
                          e.g. */c/a/t/, /h/e/n/*
Blending   –   3 and 4 phoneme words, blending together to make words
                          e.g. *c – a – t*
Exchanging   –   Substitution, deletion, recognising patterns in words
                          e.g. *cap, map, tap*

Develop an awareness of *rhyme* and *rhythm* (syllables)

- Which two rhyme?   cat/hat/dog.
- Child provides rhyming word with cat/dog/tree (inc. nonsense words).
- Play rhyme riddles, e.g. Mr Paul is very ...
- Listen and count beats in music, link this to the way we speak in rhythm.
- Clap out rhythm in a word phrase, e.g. el/e/phant, bread, but/ter (i.e. syllables).

Develop an awareness of *initial* letter sounds

- Teach how the sounds of words are formed in the mouth.
- Teach first, exaggerated sounds: f/m s/l n/r v/z.
- Ensure that children are taught to listen to the close differences in sounds,
  e.g. **p/b**   unvoiced/voiced
     t/d   "   "
     k/c/g   "   "
     s/z   "   "
     f/v   "   "
     m/n   fine discrimination of sound.
- Ensure that initial sounds are not combined with 'u' to sound like 'muh', 'luh', 'suh' as this may only hinder development of good blending skills.
- Play 'Granny went to market......' – buy something beginning with same letter.
- Give pictures to sort according to initial letter sound.
- Tongue-twisters using initial letter sounds and extend alliteration skills, e.g. **S**ammy **s**eal **s**aw a **s**eagull.
- Invent a monster that eats things beginning with '**m**' – can he eat a cat, jam? etc.
- Choose any word (e.g. from NLS text) and ask children to listen and say what sound they hear at the beginning of the word.
- Use alliteration (i.e. same sound) to help children remember short vowel sounds, e.g. 'a' apple; 'e' egg.
- Say a word, e.g. 'jam' and then say it omitting the final consonant – 'ja_' and ask children to say which letter/sound is missing.

Develop an awareness of the *initial*, *final* & *medial* sound in cvc words

- Play a game with cvc picture word cards, e.g. pan, web, cat, etc. Take turns to pick up card and ask the children to listen and identify the position of **initial**, **final** and **medial** sound. Give all children the chance to role reverse and play the teacher – this helps to develop confidence. Develop identification of the position of sounds in words until the children are fully confident in sound discrimination.

Develop an awareness of onset and *rime*

- Write the five vowels on the whiteboard in a column.
- Add a consonant after the vowel, e.g. **at**, **et**, **it**, **ot**, **ut**. Play lots of games ensuring that the children have grasped sound/symbol relationship. Continue with other consonants aiming for blending fluency.
- Write onsets on the board and ask the children to blend them with the rime 'at', e.g. b**at**, h**at**, s**at**, m**at**, etc. Nonsense words help to develop accuracy in blending. Divide onset/rime in only one place: b/**at**.

- It is very important to develop fluency in blending so that children can hear the letters blend together.
- When a child can read any word with an obvious rime pattern, teach other words that follow the pattern, e.g. sight word '**and**' leads to reading by analogy, e.g. h**and**, s**and**, b**and**.
- Use wooden/plastic letters for children to interchange onsets: **p**en/**h**en/**m**en.

Develop an awareness of blends and digraphs

- Try to teach common digraphs '**sh**', '**ch**', and '**th**' when introducing letter sounds. Contrast the difference in sound between **s/sh, jkh, f/th**. Give the children examples of the difference in meaning simply by the change of sound, e.g. **sue/shoe, jug/chug, fin/thin**.
- Teach blends thoroughly. Play lots of games that help children to gain an accurate knowledge and solid foundation to develop their word blending skills further.
- Ask children to 'track' blends on a page of print. They should use a highlighter pen and mark each time the blend appears. Encourage role reversal in games and activities.

15 Comprehension of language

Comprehension of language is also known as 'understanding' or 'receptive' language.

The following shows a normal pattern of language development and may prove a useful guideline when working with children with delayed language:

12–18 months

- Points to familiar objects on request, 'Where is teddy?' 'Where's the car?' etc.
- Follows simple commands, e.g. 'Get your coat', 'Shut the door' etc.
- Is able to show own or doll's hair, hands, shoes etc.
- Demonstrates definitions by use, e.g. brush own hair.

2–3 years

- Understands function of objects and can identify simple objects by use, e.g. 'What do we cut with?'
- Acts on simple commands with 2 key words, e.g. 'Put the box on the chair' (where there is an alternative to 'box' and 'chair').
- Can match objects to pictures.
- Can relate meaningfully to miniature toys.

3 years

- Acts upon 3–4 key words instructions, e.g.   'Put the book under the chair'
  'Put the teddy under the bed'
  (where an alternative is provided to the underlined objects).
- Understands concepts big/little/in/on/under.
- Understands some reference to past and future events.
- Understands attributes of objects, e.g. 'Which man has the biggest hat?'
- Listens to stories of increasing length.

4 years

- Understanding less based in the present, shows more developed under-standing of past and future tense.
  Acts upon 4+ key word instructions, e.g. 'Put the <u>red crayon</u> in the <u>little box</u>' (where an alternative is provided to the underlined objects).
- Understands concepts such as behind/in front of and long/short.
- Can identify some colours.

5 years

- Can understand everyday conversations.
- Understands and follows more complex instructions.
- Concept of time starts to develop, e.g. 'today', 'tomorrow' and 'yesterday'.

16 Problems arising from comprehension difficulties

The following problems may be due to difficulties with understanding spoken language. These problems may also, to varying degrees, be caused by:

Poor auditory memory
Sequencing difficulties
Immaturity of attention control
Poor auditory processing

- Difficulty following instructions.
- Unable to follow story or to answer questions, for example in English.
- Expressive language affected: may lack vocabulary or have problems with grammar and syntax.
- May find it hard to concentrate in class or to sit still.
- May be able to read accurately, but can lack understanding of text.
- May appear to have behaviour difficulties.
- May have poor self-esteem; may find it hard to socialise with other children.

17 Elements of language

Understanding may break down because children have difficulty with the following (difficulties here will also be reflected in the child's spoken language):

Vocabulary

Learnt through context and experience.

Children with vocabulary difficulties miss out on the building bricks of later language development.

Semantics

An understanding of how words link and relate to each other and how context affects words. For example: the different meanings of 'light' in the phrases 'light green' and 'a light load'.

Syntax

Following and understanding structure and word order of sentences. For example the different meanings of 'the man pushed the horse' and the more complex 'the man is being pushed by the horse'.

Morphology

The smallest element of meaning in a word, such as the 's' in 'hats' as opposed to 'hat' or the 'ed' in 'walked' as opposed to 'walk'. These endings change the meaning of language, but may not be understood by a child with comprehension difficulty.

---

18 General strategies to help improve language comprehension

- Use child's name and establish eye contact before speaking.
- Encourage active listening (see 'Listening skills' section starting on page 14).
- Ensure that activities are appropriate for child's level of development, e.g. use real objects in preference to line drawings for younger children.
- When teaching verbs, ask the children to perform the actions and to use the words that describe them.
- Use everyday objects that reflect the child's experience.
- Vary objects and activities to maintain interest.
- Ensure a lot of practice and reinforcement of new vocabulary and concepts.
- Use in a variety of situations to encourage the child to generalise skills. Remember, it may take a long time to learn new concepts and words.
- Adult's speech should be clear and unhurried, with normal intonation.
- Keep sentences short, if necessary broken into separate parts.
- Re-phrase sentences.
- Allow time for the child to respond.
- When reading with the child, talk about the story; ask what? where? or who? questions to establish understanding.
- At a higher level, ask why? how? or when? questions about stories, objects or events.
- Use role play to help children understand why or when they are having difficulty understanding. For example, play a barrier game and do not give the child all the necessary information to complete a task.
- Encourage the child to tell you when they do not understand.
- Offer a range of options: ask for clarification, use a dictionary, re-read a text (looking at contextual cues) or ask a neighbour.
- Use visual cues to support spoken information and, if appropriate, use gesture or signing to accompany language.

19 The use of visual supports to aid understanding

Children who experience difficulties with communication may need visual strategies to aid their understanding. Images can provide a two-way communication path for anyone who has limited verbal abilities.

Tod and Blamires (1998) suggest that learners may need to have the following visual cues emphasised as they may not be able to make as much use of them as accomplished communicators.

Body language

e.g. facial expression, body posture and proximity, touching, eye contact, direction and shifting of gaze.

Environmental cues

e.g. signs, labels, written messages, instructions, notes, furniture arrangement, location and movement of people and objects.

Tools for giving information and helping organisation

e.g. calendars, daily planners, schedules, shopping lists, notes, menus, maps.

Specially designed tools for specific needs

✔ *Schedules and mini-schedules* – outlining the day or part of the day. They may be for all the class to use or for a specific child who may have the schedule by his/her desk.
✔ *Choice boards* – showing a range of choices.
✔ *Task organisers* – step by step prompts to help a learner complete a task. This may include individualised worksheets that show what the task is, what materials are required, the stages of the task and how it will be finished. It is recommended that traditionally established organising principles be used to structure tasks, e.g. left to right and top down.

Label prompts in the environment

Support may be required to help the child make use of existing visual cues, e.g. exit signs, toilets, etc. The child may need the additional support of labelling areas and items. Having a place for everything and returning it to its place can be made more explicit through the use of additional labelled containers and/or marked out areas or boundaries, e.g. the carpeted area is a place for listening to stories or reading quietly.

Digital photographs

Digital cameras are useful as a quick and relatively simple way of providing photographs. These can be used as a guide to an activity or task showing each stage or just the completion. Photographs need to indicate the key element to be considered.

Visual communication links

Lists/pictures that communicate information from one setting to another, e.g. between home and school.

Using technology

Using mobile devices and applications (apps) can prove a valuable way of motivating children to develop their speech and language skills. The Appendix contains a list of apps, websites and games that can be used as rewards.

Picture or object exchange systems

This involves exchange of a picture or object referring to a desired item with the teacher, who immediately responds to the request. An example of a picture communication system is *PECS* or *Picture Exchange Communication System* (see 'Resources' section).

20 Expressive language (spoken)

The following shows a normal pattern of expressive or spoken language development:

12–18 months

- Child uses 2–20 recognisable words.
- Uses one word to express whole idea.
- May use echolalia, i.e. echoes last or prominent word said to him/her.
- Communicates wishes by pointing.

2–3 years

- Vocabulary increases to 200+ but speech will show signs of immature sentence structure or phonology (sound system).
- What? Where? and who? questions are emerging.
- Uses simple 2–3 word sentences, e.g. 'Daddy kick ball';
                                              'Put dolly bath'.

3–4 years

- Sentences become more complex: using prepositions, adjectives, plurals and some use of past tense.
- Starting to ask why? when? and who? questions.
- Can carry on simple conversations.
- Is able to talk about recent events and experiences.
- Can recite simple nursery rhymes.
- Will play imaginatively and comment on what is happening.
- May experience periods of normal non-fluency in speech production.

4–5 years

- Sentences grammatically correct and intelligible.
- A few speech substitutions remain (e.g. /r/ to /w/ and /th/ to /f/).
- Can give a connected account of recent events and experiences.
- Knows various rhymes and jingles.
- Enjoys jokes and playing with language.
- Often asks why/what/where/when/how? questions.
- Likes to ask the meanings of words.

5 years

- Speech is fluent, grammatically correct and usually phonetically correct.
- Enjoys singing and reciting nursery rhymes.
- Constantly asking the meaning of abstract words and uses them with delight.
- Enjoys jokes and riddles.

21 Problems arising from expressive language difficulties

- Child may be withdrawn and isolated.
- May have difficulty establishing friendships.
- May have poor eye contact and turn-taking skills.
- May be frustrated and appear to have behaviour difficulties.
- Sentence structure may appear immature; word order may be confused.
- May use gesture and 'empty' words such as 'that' or 'thingy'.
- Unable to join in class discussions or to answer questions.
- Will be unable to make needs or worries known.
- May have literacy difficulties as written language will reflect spoken language.
- May have difficulty with prediction, sequencing and inference.

22 General strategies to help expressive language difficulties

- Check hearing.
- Check child's understanding.
- Observe the child, see where and when s/he talks spontaneously.
- The child may need a warm, close relationship with an adult to encourage him/her to talk.
- Do not expect spontaneous talk in all situations until confident in familiar ones.
- Use concrete objects and familiar events and objects to talk about.
- Give the child full attention when s/he wants to speak.
- Give child time to talk.
- Record samples of the child's language and where appropriate complete an assessment (see 'Resources' section for suggestions on assessments). Seek specialist help if appropriate.
- Comment on activities, talk while playing or working alongside the child, encourage communication.
- Use corrective feedback, but do not pressurise the child to repeat what may be difficult.
- Use signing or gesture to augment communication.
- Use categorisation to help child develop word-finding skills.

23 Specific strategies to develop expressive language skills

The following techniques can be used to elicit specific vocabulary or sentence structures:

✔ Modelled imitation
✔ Forced alternatives
✔ Indirect modelling
✔ Cloze procedure
✔ Expansion
✔ Role reversal
✔ Obstacle presentation

Modelled imitation

- The adult models language for the child to imitate, for example:
  If you would like juice say 'juice please'.
- Use the language to be copied at the end of the sentence to help memory.
- Signs can be used to accompany language where necessary.

Forced alternatives

This will give the child vocabulary that is needed, but is not simple imitation:

N.B. The target phrase or word should always be given first to avoid the child simply echoing the last word they heard.
(a) Help with word finding retrieval, e.g.
   Adult: **What colour is the apple?**
   Child: **No response.**
   Adult: **Is it green or blue?**
   Child: **Green.**
(b) Help with incorrect productions, e.g.
   Child: **Me want a turn.**
   Adult: **Do you say me want a turn or I want a turn?**
   Child: **I want a turn.**
(c) Help with expanding sentence structure, e.g:
   Child: **Girl eat.**
   Adult: **Is it girl eating an apple or girl eating a cake?**
   Child: **Girl eat cake.**

Indirect modelling

Here the adult produces a statement in such a way as to indirectly provide the child with the words s/he will need.

This relies on the child actively analysing the model and reproducing it or aspects of it in their speech.

It is useful for prompting passive children into making requests, e.g.

Adult: **If you want more juice, ask me.**
Child: **Want more juice.**
Adult: **Tell me if you need a pencil.**
Child: **Need pencil.**
Adult: **If you ask me, where is the rubber? I will tell you.**
Child: **Where is the rubber?**

Cloze procedure

Here the adult models a sentence and prompts the child to use a similar sentence but with a different vocabulary:

Two pictures: a boy eating a cake and a girl eating an apple.

Adult: **This is a girl eating an apple and this is...**
Child: **Boy eat cake.**
Adult: **I'm sitting on a big chair and you're sitting...**
Child: **On little chair.**

Expansion

The adult reinforces and expands upon what the child has said. The aim is not for the child to reproduce the adult's expanded version but to experience language at a slightly higher level than they have been using, e.g:

Child: **Daddy car.**
Adult: **That's right, daddy's gone in the car.**
Child: **We wented to the park.**
Adult: **Yes, we went to the park yesterday.**

Rolel reversal

Here the adult models the language first. Then the adult and child swap roles and the child is encouraged to use the same or similar commands, e.g:

Adult: **Put the teddy in the box.**
      Put the pencil under the table.
      Now you tell me what to do.

Obstacle presentation

The adult sets up a situation which forces the child to make some form of comment or request, e.g:

The adult gives the child a puzzle to complete, but some pieces are missing.

The adult asks the child to cut out a picture, but does not provide any scissors.

24 Social communication difficulties in children

Some children have difficulty with understanding and using language effectively to communicate. They may have problems in the following areas:

- The child has difficulty interacting with peers and may appear to be detached from the group.
- The child's expressive language may be in advance of their understanding.
- The child's language or responses may, however, appear inappropriate at times; s/he may change topic without warning or use stereotyped utterances.
- The child may not have naturally absorbed the norms of social etiquette. For example, s/he may talk to adults in an over-familiar way, may stand too close to another person or inappropriately touch them.
- The child may find turn-taking difficult in: conversation, e.g. may talk over another and not listen to questions; games/activities, e.g. may be unwilling to share, dislike losing.
- The child may experience difficulty with eye contact and inattention may be a problem. S/he may fail to pick up on non-verbal cues, such as facial expression or tone of voice, e.g. the child may not realise that someone who is frowning is annoyed.
- The child may learn to read at an early age, but s/he may have a poor understanding of what s/he has read.
- The child may have difficulty with inference and predicting and seeing things from another person's perspective.
- The child may fail to see the overall picture and tend to concentrate on the smaller details instead.
- The child's language may be highly literal so that sarcasm, jokes and idioms are not clearly understood, e.g. 'Pull your socks up'.
- The child may have difficulty with abstract language and time concepts, e.g. child may be confused if s/he is told 'you can play a game when you have finished your work' (see 'Resources' section for recommendations).

25 General strategies to help children with social communication difficulties

- Listen to the child, giving time to talk, do not answer on his/her behalf.
- Give gentle reminders if communication skills have broken down.
- Talk about events or difficulties as they arise.
- Guide the child towards solving his/her own problems.
- Talk about how the child is feeling and how others may feel in a given situation.
- Give the child choices and let him/her tell you which s/he wants.
- Use visual cues and prompts where possible.
- Use real objects and materials wherever appropriate to demonstrate.

26 Specific activities: Early Years and Key Stage 1

The young child with social communication difficulties may appear to be talking well; much of his/her language, however, may be simply memorised chunks, used without full understanding. The child needs to start using language to communicate. The following recommendations are taken from *Semantic-Pragmatic Language Disorder* by Firth and Venkatesh (see Resources) and provides very useful practical strategies:

Following and giving instructions

An important area for understanding the language of the classroom.

- Play Simon Says or other PE activities, where child has to run, jump, stop, stand still etc. on request. In appropriate situations, child can instruct adult or group of children.
- Play alongside child with toys, instruct child to 'put dolly's hat on' or to 'put teddy's shoes on'. Keep language simple, expand as child's understanding develops. Reverse roles and child instructs adult.
- Child and adult have identical drawing, barrier between the two. Adult instructs child to add/colour objects on picture; compare the pictures to see accuracy of results. Reverse roles and child instructs adult.

Confirming and refuting (saying yes/no)

Some children find this hard and have a tendency to say 'yes' to everything you ask them.

- Pick up objects and ask the child, 'is this an apple?' etc.
- Sort coloured cubes, asking the child if a cube is a certain colour or not.
- Sort items belonging to different people, 'Is this Sam's?' etc.

Requesting and listening to requests

Again a vital area if the child is to function in the classroom and interact with peers.
- Play fishing game, where child has to request specific items and retrieve them. Reverse roles.
- Play at shopping; ask the child for items; develop level of complexity from 'cake please' to 'please can I have a cake' when appropriate. Child takes turn at being shopkeeper.
- Play game together, adult asks for parts of jigsaw/construction toy and encourages child to do the same.

Asking and answering questions

An understanding of 'wh' questions is vital in the development of understanding language.
- Child hides a toy in the room and adult asks questions about its whereabouts; child and adult then reverse roles.
- Give the child a choice of drinks or biscuits and ask which s/he would like. Allow the child to give out food or drink to group and to ask the children what they want.
- Use a feely bag and encourage the child to ask what things are; ask questions about what an object feels like etc.
- Look at a picture book together and ask the child questions about what s/he can see, for example, 'where is the boy' etc.

Turn-taking skills

This is an important pre-linguistic skill and one which some children need to learn specifically.
- Play circle activities, pass round a bean bag and ask the child to say name whilst holding the bean bag. Increase complexity of language when appropriate.
- Play dice/board games, at first adult and child and then, if appropriate with two or three children. Ensure that each child takes turns, ask at intervals, 'whose turn is it next?'

Specific grammatical areas

In order to develop a child's language, it may be useful to focus on specific areas. This will encourage the child to start using language appropriately, rather than simply repeating memorised chunks.

- **Nouns:** Ask the child to name objects, photos or pictures; this can be done in a game context, such as fishing, lotto or shopping.
- **Verbs:** Ask the child to perform certain actions and to describe what actions others are doing. Use verb photos or pictures as nouns, above.
- **Adjectives:** Feel and describe toys, such as 'fluffy cat', 'soft teddy' or 'bouncy ball'.
- **Prepositions:** Use small toys and place items in/on/under another, e.g. 'put the shoes in the cupboard', 'put the doll under the bed' etc.

27 Specific activities: Key Stage 2

The child now needs to learn to communicate with other children as well as adults. The previous activities for Key Stage 1 started to use these skills and the child would now benefit from wider experience with peers.

Turn-taking and verbal and non-verbal communication skills

Develop the ideas used in circle time activities for younger children:

- Take it in turns in circle time to talk about such topics as food, family, pets etc.
- When children are more confident in circle time, talk about feelings and emotions in different situations, e.g. 'how do you feel when you are going to the dentist/cinema, get a present' etc.

Rules of conversation

Just as other children need to be taught reading and spelling, so some will need to be taught the rules of conversation, as they do not pick them up incidentally.

- Two adults can act out a conversation, making a series of mistakes, which the children have to spot, for example:
  - Talking too fast.
  - Not listening to other person/talking over them.
  - Not looking at other person.
  - Standing too close to the other person.
  - Changing the subject too often and without warning.

The children can then devise a list of conversational rules that will serve as a reminder for them at a later date.

© 2015, *Supporting Children with Speech and Learning Difficulties*
Allenby, Fearon-Wilson, Merrison and Morling, Routledge

Using appropriate language/questions

The following activities will help the child to use language accurately and appropriately:

- Use barrier games, as for younger children, but with instructions of increasing complexity. Instead of a child and an adult, two children can work together, taking it in turns to instruct the other person.
- One child instructs another to draw a similar picture, for example, of a monster/alien. They compare drawings afterwards to see how successful they have been.
- One child hides an object and the second child has to ask appropriate questions to find out where it is.
- One child has a picture of an object and the other has to work out what it is from a series of questions, for example 'where do you find it?' or 'who would use it?' etc.
- As above, but this time the questions can only be answered 'yes' or 'no'. For example, 'is it alive?' or 'is it an animal?' etc. This will encourage the children to think in terms of categories and classification.

Inference and prediction

These activities will encourage children to think of language in terms other than the literal and the concrete.

- In story sessions/English lessons encourage the child to predict what will happen in a story.
- Ask 'why' s/he feels something has happened, for example, 'why is Sam wearing a coat and hat?' (because it is cold).
- Encourage the child to relate to the feelings of others through story; 'How do you think Sam felt when he saw his friend fall out of the tree?' Help the child to find words for emotions beyond simply 'happy' or 'sad'.
- Use sequence pictures, but with the final picture not revealed. Talk about the events in the pictures and ask the child to suggest what might happen next.

Understanding of time/sequencing

The concept of time is a complex one for many children to appreciate, particularly those children with social communication difficulties.

- The child may benefit from a visual timetable where each activity of the day is represented in picture form. When an activity is finished, it could be placed in the 'finished box' (see section on 'The use of visual supports').
- As the child becomes more familiar with this, clock faces could be put next to each activity to show when each was (theoretically) going to happen.
- Questions could be asked, such as 'At what time do we do PE?' or 'What do we do after assembly?'
- Take photographs of the child in a series of actions, for example, coming into school, hanging up coat, putting away packed lunch, going into classroom and sitting down. Use these to generate language and the idea of sequenced activities.
- Use commercially produced sequence cards, as above. Ask the child, for example, 'What happens in the first picture/after the boy got home/what did he do before he saw the dog?' etc.
- Carry out a task that requires a sequence of actions, for example, making a sandwich; talk about what was done, make picture representations and ask the child to make a sandwich following the picture cues.
- For time concepts involving longer passages of time, such as the growth of plants, show the children stages of growth at one time, for example, the hyacinth bulb in the soil, the pot with the small shoot, the taller shoot and the flower in bloom. Ask them to put the pots in sequence. Talk about how long it would take for the plant to grow.

Specific grammatical areas

The children may need to practise the following:

Past tense:
- Ask the children to close their eyes and listen to the adult performing an action, such as clapping hands. They then open their eyes and say what happened: 'you clapped your hands.' etc.
- Use picture sequences to describe, where the child has to tell what has happened in the pictures, e.g. 'he picked the flowers' etc.
- In the English lesson, ask the child to tell what has happened in a story, modelling language where necessary.

Future tense:
- Show the children a half-completed action, such as a ball about to be kicked, a door about to be shut. Say to the children, 'what will I do?' and they should say, 'you are going to shut the door'. Once again, the language may need to be modelled and the children encouraged not to simply answer, 'shut the door'.
- Use sequencing cards/pictures and ask the children what is going to happen, encouraging responses, as above.

Adjectives:
- Develop understanding and use of adjectives by using feely bags, where the child has to describe what they can feel.
- Alternatively, the children ask the child who is touching the object what it feels like, 'Is it soft/hard?' etc.
- Play a board game, when the child lands on a certain square, they have to think of/find an object that is: heavy, red, wooden, soft etc.

Building vocabulary

Many children lack a breadth of vocabulary or have word-finding difficulties. They would benefit from the following:

Categorisation skills: this is useful, both as a way of enriching language and of helping children with word-finding difficulties to access words from their memory.

- Play a game where the children have to collect pictures from a certain category. Talk about the category and think of other objects from it.
- The adult thinks of a category and the children have to come up with items from that category.
- Collect pairs of items/pictures of items that go together, such as knife and fork, toothpaste and toothbrush, talk about why they go together.
- Ask the child to select the odd one out from a series of items/pictures. This involves the child understanding categorisation in order to understand and then explain why an item is different from the rest.

28 Circle time

Circle time is a time for children to gather together to share their ideas and feelings and to discuss matters of significance.

It can provide a good opportunity for helping children with language difficulties to develop the following areas:

✔ Attention control
✔ Turn-taking skills
✔ Eye contact
✔ Social interaction
✔ Self-esteem
✔ Good listening
✔ Good speaking
✔ Good thinking.

To do this, it is important to establish ground rules.

Ground rules for circle time

- Everyone is equal (it helps if you all sit at the same level).
- Everyone should have the chance to speak (it may help to pass around an object for the speaker to hold).
- Each person has a responsibility to listen.
- Everyone shows respect for another's point of view.
- Children have a right not to speak if they so wish.
- Children should not be penalised when they choose not to speak.
- Children should not be excluded from circle time for previous inappropriate behaviour.

The teacher will need to:
- Set the rules as above, which are, in essence, good listening skills, with respect for others' points of view.
- Find a suitable time.
- Praise good listening skills.
- Explain that what is talked about in circle time is confidential.
- Plan variety within the sessions; introduce enjoyable routines to start and end with.
- Build self-evaluation into the circle time.

29 Activities for circle time

There are several publications which provide ideas for circle time activities, for example, *Language Development: Circle Time Sessions to Improve Communication Skills* by Nash, Lowe and Palmer, and for secondary pupils, *Quality Circle Time in the Secondary School: A Handbook of Good Practice* by Mosley and Tew.

As a general rule, where a circle time activity involves talking, pass round an object such as a beanbag or a soft toy, which the speaker can hold. Activities can include some of the following:

Sentence completion

- 'My name is...'
- 'I like to...'
- 'My favourite lesson is...'

Passing an action

- Pass around a clap or series of claps.
- Stand up in turn around the circle.
- Look at the person next to you in turn.
- Pass around you a smile.
- Decide on a feeling, such as 'happy' or 'angry' and pass around a face to go with that feeling. This is a useful activity for children with social communication difficulties.

Passing an object

- Passing a beanbag or ball around the circle is a simple and effective warm up activity for children with difficulties with turn-taking or immature attention control.
- Joining hands and passing a hula hoop around the circle (either over heads or under feet) is a good team building activity which requires the group to work together.

Discussing topics

- Talk about areas of interest or concern to the group, such as bullying or school rules.
- For older children, this might include topics such as politics, drugs and alcohol.

Problem-solving

- Some children have used circle time as a useful opportunity to talk about problems that have arisen.
- Differences can be talked about and possible solutions aired as a group.
- Stories can be used to refer to ways of dealing with problems.

30 Citizenship through circle time

Circle time offers a very useful opportunity to put the ideals of citizenship into practice. It models the qualities that the curriculum seeks to promote.

Circle time can offer children with speech and language difficulties the opportunity to practise skills they may have problems with and to see those skills modelled by other children.

These include:

- Co-operation and turn-taking.
- Active and supportive listening.
- Sharing and managing feelings.
- Affirmation of self and others. Developing empathy.
- Communicating ideas and opinions.
- Voting on issues. Considering some political and topical issues.
- Making real choices and decisions, such as school rules, in the class and the playground.
- Looking at the qualities of friendship.
- Reflective thinking. Setting and reviewing goals.
- Considering moral dilemmas. Taking action.

31 Speech acquisition

A normally developing pattern of speech acquisition would be broadly as follows:

Age	Sounds acquired
18 months	m n p b t d w and vowels
2–2.5 years	as above plus k g ng h and vowels
2–3.5 years	Starting to use f, s, l, and y (as in 'you')
3 years	As above plus z l and vowels
4 years	As above plus ch j and vowels
5 years	Starting to develop r th Speech fully understandable.

Delay or disorder?

A child's speech is considered to be **delayed** when their progress follows a normal pattern, but their speech sound acquisition is that of a younger child.

A child's phonology is considered **disordered** when the processes used are inconsistent and not following the normal pattern of phonological development (as seen above).

32 Speech difficulties

School age children whose speech is still unclear in any of the following areas would be considered to be *delayed*:

- **Fronting:** a sound which should be produced at the back of the mouth is made further forward:
    Cat can become **tat**
    Get can become **det**
    Sing can become **sin** or **sim**.

- **Stopping of fricatives:** the longer fricative sounds (f, v, s, z, sh, th) become short plosive sounds (p, b, t, d, k):
    Sun can become **tun**
    Fan can become **pan**.

- **Cluster reduction:** the child leaves out consonant sounds from a cluster, most commonly l, r or s:
    Skate can become **Kate** or **sate**
    Spot can become **pot** or **sot**.

- **Final consonant deletion:** here the final consonant is not sounded:
    Tent can become **ten**
    Milk can become **mil**.

The following is **not** part of normal development and would be considered a possible indication of a **language disorder**.

- **Backing:** the opposite of fronting; the sound is made further back in the mouth:
    Pan can become **can**
    Tap can become **cap**
    Bet can become **get**.

33 Points to note when working with children with speech and language difficulties

- If a child has speech problems, it is very important to refer him/her to a speech and language therapist who can discuss the difficulties.
- Establishing links between the school, home and the therapist is a useful way of using different people's skills and knowledge. It is the most effective way of helping the child.
- It is important to establish the child's ability to discriminate between sounds as this is necessary before s/he can alter his/her own production.
- Do remember that a child who has phonological problems will not be able to use sounds which are beyond his/her developmental level (see chart, above).
- The child may not be consistent in sound substitution. If this is the case or if many sounds are affected, then his/her speech may be very difficult to understand.
- The difficulty the child has with particular sounds may depend on that sound's position within a word and on the sounds adjacent to it. For example, s/he may be able to sound /k/ in 'cup', but cannot sound in 'back'.

34 Classroom strategies for helping children with speech difficulties

A. Locke and M. Beech in *Teaching Talking* recommend the following:

- Check the child's hearing.
- Check understanding.
- Listen to the child; his/her speech will become more comprehensible with familiarity.
- Remember to use context and present experience.
- Encourage the child to watch and listen to the person talking to them.
- Encourage the child to talk slowly in short sentences.
- Avoid allowing the child to talk on and on; try asking questions to help clarify what s/he wants to say.
- Encourage the child to make him/herself understood by using gesture, drawings, own signs, etc.
- Do not ask the child to repeat what s/he has said or to say a particular word properly.

35 Language in the Early Years Foundation Stage

> Communication is critical to improving a child's life chances, giving them the social skills they need to achieve at school, understand their teachers, make friends and ultimately give them the best start in life.
>
> (I CAN 2013)

The Early Years Foundation Stage (EYFS) which sets standards for the learning, development and care of children from birth to 5 years old, takes heed of this. It places language development at its centre.

The EYFS focuses on the three prime and four specific areas of learning most essential for children's readiness for future learning and healthy development.

The prime areas are:

- **Personal, social and emotional development**
- **Communication and language**
- **Physical development.**

Communication and language is divided into three areas:

- **Listening and attention**
- **Understanding**
- **Speaking.**

It involves giving children opportunities to experience a language rich environment, where they can gain confidence, express themselves and interact with others.

Each of the areas covered is tracked through from birth to 60 months plus (see pages 7, 24–25 and 31–32 for stages of development).

36 Strategies for developing spoken language

Literacy unites the important skills of reading and writing. It also involves speaking and listening, which although they are not separately identified in the framework, are an essential part of it. Good oral work enhances pupils' understanding of language in both oral and written forms and of the way language can be used to communicate. (DfEE 1998)

Speaking and listening is the foundation of written work. Children need to be able to use language orally before they can be expected to produce it in written form. They need to be able to use language to develop their thinking and reasoning skills and to access the curriculum.

In view of this the QCA has issued guidance entitled *Speaking, Listening, Learning: Working with Children in Key Stages 1 and 2* (2003). This document looks at language across the curriculum and sets objectives for speaking and listening in Years 1 to 6.

The following recommendations will help to provide ideas for English lessons.

Strategies for developing spoken language in Literacy

- Sit the child near you where s/he can follow the visual cues of other children.
- Use the child's name frequently.
- Encourage good eye contact.
- Gain the child's full attention when engaged in talk or discussion (see section on 'Teaching "Active Listening"').
- Use simple sentences; avoid complicated sentence structures, such as the passive or abstract vocabulary and concepts.
- Encourage the child, where appropriate, to answer in full sentences,
  e.g.   Teacher: 'Where is the dog hiding?'
            Child: The dog is hiding under the table.'
- Using object prompts will help promote greater understanding, e.g. story sacks or any objects or artefacts which are part of the text.
- Picture prompts will also help understanding and will support new vocabulary.
- Relate the text to the children's experience whenever possible.
- Use varied strategies, such as direct modelling or forced alternatives to elicit responses from the child (see Expressive Language section on 'Specific Strategies to Develop Expressive Language Skills').

- Circle time can be incorporated into English developing either:
  - ✔ skills such as turn-taking, eye contact and social interaction;
  - ✔ specific speech and language objectives.
- Allow the child the opportunity to develop their language. This will involve giving them time to reply and perhaps, at times, suppressing more vocal class members.
- The child who is hesitant may prefer to whisper their answer to a child support assistant before they talk to the whole class.
- Ensure that 'wh' questions are used appropriately.
- Use sign prompts, where appropriate, to help develop understanding.

Use of questions

'Wh' questions are vital for an understanding of the language of the classroom. For the child with language difficulties, it is better to start with simpler questions, such as:

'What?'	e.g. 'What is in the tree?' (bird)
	'What is the girl doing?' (girl running)
	The expected answer can be a noun or a verb or a simple phrase.
'Where?'	e.g. 'Where is the man?' (in the car)
	Encourage the child not to simply point or answer 'there', but to use early prepositions, such as in/on/under etc.
'Who?'	e.g. 'Who has a big ice cream?' (Sam).

When the child can understand the above, you can move to:

'Why?'	e.g. 'Why is the boy crying?' (he fell over).
'How?'	e.g. 'How do we know it's raining outside?' (because he's wet).
'When?'	e.g. 'When do we go on the computer?' (after play).

Written language in English

Children with spoken language difficulties may have strong visual skills and these can be used to good advantage.
- Give the child the object they are to write about, let him/her look at it and feel it to help generate language.
- Use simple picture sequences as a framework for writing. Ask the child to sequence the pictures and to talk about what is happening in them.
- Use computers to generate picture sequences, where the child can either match sentences to pictures or write his/her own sentences.

Children with language difficulties can benefit greatly from developing their reading skills; this will provide them with a starting point from which comprehension and language use can be extended.

- Use High Frequency words to generate sentences which can, in turn, develop spoken language skills:

    e.g. 'I can ....'
    'I like ...'
    'I can see a ....' etc.

- Use the child's own reading book to enhance the child's use of language. Develop skills such as understanding of cause and effect, empathy and ability to predict or imagine. This will be particularly important for children with social communication difficulties (see section on 'Social Communication').

37 Language and Mathematics

Oral work is a key part of Maths work.

A balance of whole class teaching and group work plays a central role in the learning process.

Do remember:

Many children with language and learning difficulties have problems with **sequencing**, which is vital for the development of mathematical concepts.

They may also have problems understanding **cause and effect**, which is another important area in mathematical understanding.

Children with problems of **short-term auditory memory** will have difficulty with mental maths. They may need to develop prompts and strategies to help them, such as visualising or using their fingers.

Children with language difficulties will need time and a lot of practice in order to acquire a **mathematical vocabulary**.

✔ Ensure that the child understands what s/he is being asked to do. For the child with language difficulties, **concepts** such as more and less, before and after, smaller and larger than, may need explaining and lots of practical activities carried out before knowledge becomes secure.

✔ Ensure that **vocabulary**, as well as concepts, is familiar, so that the children know, for example, what a triangle, or a corner, or a side is. Use appropriate displays, with visual prompts, for the children to refer to during lessons.

✔ When asking the whole class a question, build in enough '**wait time**' to allow all children to think of their answer. Ask the whole class to repeat a correct answer, using a **complete sentence**.

✔ Wherever possible, allow the child access to **concrete apparatus** so that s/he can develop concepts and vocabulary through practical experience.

✔ An '**empty number line**' helps children to structure and record mental processes. It is a useful aid to short-term memory.

✔ Try to relate learning to **real life experience**, so that maths is not seen as simply a school subject, but rather as something of practical and everyday use.

38 The management of communication problems in the classroom

(Strategies taken from *Teaching Talking* by A. Locke and M. Beech.)

Regular use of appropriate management strategies can be very beneficial in fostering communication skills in children. Here are some general management strategies for all children identified with problems in communication:

Increasing confidence

a) Relationships with adults
b) Relationships with other children
c) Being successful.

a) *Relationships with adults*

- Make a point of having a relaxed 'chat' with the child.
- Chat during practical activities.
- Adults should always pause to show they would welcome a response from the child.

b) *Relationships with other children*

- Put the child with others who communicate well but who will not dominate the conversation.

c) *Being successful*

- Develop all skills but especially where the child shows special interest or ability.
- Regularly show appreciation of the child's effort.

Helping communication in the classroom

a) Noise level
b) Context
c) Watching and listening
d) Other children
e) Parents
f) Repetition
g) Collecting background information.

a) Noise level

- Have quiet areas in the classroom where the child can spend part of the day listening or talking with an adult with or without other children.

b) Context

- Shared context and experiences are easier to talk about than events that are only known to one person.

c) Watching and listening

- Encourage the child to give eye contact.
- Encourage the child to watch as well as listen.
- Say name to gain attention.

d) Other children

- Can be helpful by repeating instructions, explaining or demonstrating tasks.
- N.B. Care should be taken that someone else does not always talk for the child.

e) Parents

- Share information from home so that school can talk about home experiences.
- A home–school book may be useful – messages can be written, pictures drawn and interesting events described.

f) Repetition

- Rhymes, poems, songs thus attending to speech patterns, new vocabulary and language structures.
- Learning to listen well to stories.

g) Collecting background information

- Outside agencies, e.g. speech therapy, medical, etc.

h) Signing

- Where a child is learning to sign to aid communication, the other children in the class can practise signing too.

39 Pupils with speech, language and communication difficulties (SLCD) in secondary schools

> A pupil's level of speech, language and communication skills will have a huge impact on how well s/he copes with secondary school. Academic success will depend to a very great extent on proficiency in speaking (to different audiences), listening and reading with understanding, and writing coherently; all of these skills have to be applied across a wide range of subject areas. Over and above this, language is the basis for learning and remembering, and for developing higher order thinking skills such as planning, reasoning and reflecting.

Social and emotional well-being can also be dependent to some extent on the ability to communicate, to organise oneself and to make friends – personal skills that can be under-developed in pupils with speech, language and communication difficulties (SLCD).

Transition

For pupils who have struggled through primary school without a great deal of success or enjoyment, starting secondary school can represent a new beginning and opportunities for making better progress. But it presents new challenges too:

- The greater degree of learner-independence that is expected.
- Necessary movement around a large building.
- Constantly changing staff with their individual preferences about how work is presented, etc.

Young people with SLC difficulties, whose self-confidence may be shaky at best, may be especially 'at risk' of feeling overwhelmed.

Supporting the transition process

- Primary staff should share relevant information with secondary colleagues about any SLCD identified (even suspected).
- Interventions that have been used (even if a 'special programme' was implemented in the early years or Key Stage 1) should be discussed.
- Allocate a 'buddy', an older, responsible pupil to help to steer the newcomer through the early weeks, answer queries and generally support him or her on a day to day basis.

- Be aware that a significant number of eleven-year-olds continue to experience speech and language difficulties.
- A child's difficulties and resulting frustration may have resulted in negative behaviour; the primary school will have picked up on this – but not necessarily on the underlying causes.
- Some pupils with SLCD cover up their difficulties by 'keeping their heads down' and not drawing attention to themselves: these children are often among the 'underachievers'. Self-esteem is likely to be low at a time when adolescence can undermine it further.

Identifying SLCD

Some eleven-year-olds with SLCD will begin secondary school without having previously been identified as having SLCD. Teachers should be alert to the signs of a pupil who has SLCD and may have difficulties with:

- listening to and understanding information and instructions;
- planning and structuring their work;
- using phonics effectively for decoding (reading) and spelling (writing);
- learning technical vocabulary and using words appropriately;
- using 'academic' language (e.g. 'precis', 'analyse', 'evaluate');
- making sense of concepts they are learning;
- answering questions (they may know the answer but be unable to put it into an appropriate form of words – spoken or written);
- sharing their ideas with others;
- using language to prepare for writing or solving problems;
- asking for help or further explanation;
- interacting with others; working collaboratively and socialising.

40 Some general strategies for subject teachers

How teachers create appropriate learning environments for pupils with SLCD in different subject areas, can make all the difference to their levels of achievement.

- Ensure that the pupil sits where s/he can clearly see the teacher and the white board, where there can be frequent monitoring.
- Use his/her name at the beginning of a question or direct instruction.
- Make eye contact with the pupil while talking to him/her.
- Speak clearly and give instructions one at a time, in sequential order (avoid for example, 'before you put your books away, look at your work and underline the key vocabulary you have used today').
- Allow sufficient time for cognitive processing. Giving pupils time to process and understand information is crucial, as is time for them to formulate their answers to questions.
- Avoid ambiguity and be aware that pupils with language difficulties may not understand idioms, sarcasm or jokes based on wordplay.
- Use gesture and body language to reinforce the spoken language.
- Use pictures, diagrams, signs and other visual aids and provide an *aide memoire* for pupils as they engage in their tasks.
- Acknowledge and praise 'good listening'.
- Check understanding by asking the pupil to explain (perhaps to another learner, or a TA) what has to be done, or what has been learned.
- Pre-teach new vocabulary and concepts (use parent help at home, or a TA). This boosts confidence and enables the pupil to participate more fully and to achieve more in class.
- Encourage pupils to ask for help or clarification when needed, perhaps using a mutually agreed signal rather than 'hands up', e.g. a red card turned up on the table.
- Assign a responsible partner to work with a pupil with SLCD.

41 Secondary pupils with SLCD: Literacy

By the time SLCD pupils reach Key Stage 3 they may have experienced a lot of failure with reading and have no confidence in their abilities where text is concerned. They may have struggled with phonics and been unable to use semantics effectively when trying to work out what is on the page.

Intervention to improve reading at this stage can be very effective if it is:

- well planned;
- age appropriate; and
- carefully monitored.

Consider the following:

- A number of programmes are available to support interventions, but as with any skill, plenty of practice will help.
- Nominating a mentor for an individual pupil – perhaps a volunteer from the community, a governor or a local business employee (remember to provide training). This person will need to be patient and understanding but also be able to enthuse the pupil about books and reading.
- 'Paired reading' where the adult and pupil read together until the pupil feels confident enough to have a go by himself/herself. Taking turns to read alternate pages.
- Reading silently and then talking about the story, characters, interesting words/ facts, etc.
- Have good quality, age-appropriate books to work with, as well as newspapers and magazines.
- Ensure that the library has a good 'quick reads' section.
- Check classroom/form room reading boxes for appropriate titles.
- Include audio books.
- Poems and plays are popular for reading aloud.

42 Subject teachers supporting pupils' reading

In secondary schools, staff are usually less familiar with strategies for developing reading skills than colleagues teaching younger children. The SENCO should help to develop classroom strategies to run alongside intervention work being delivered by support staff.

Consider the following as starting points for CPD or as a handout:

- Provide regular opportunities for non-threatening reading practice, with a partner, or following text while the teacher reads. Point out any tricky words and explain what they mean.
- Build in preparation time before asking strugglers to read aloud in class; if they have practised and the passage is short, their successful reading aloud can develop self-confidence.
- Develop phonic skills and encourage pupils to sound out words using phonemes and phonic rules.
- Use a problem-solving approach to the reading of an unfamiliar word by thinking about context and grammar as well (remember there are many words which look the same but sound different, e.g. rough, plough, dough, cough; and some that sound the same but look different).
- Check for understanding; SLCD pupils can sometimes read aloud quite competently but gain only a partial understanding of what has been read.
- Provide accessible texts: short sentences, pictorial support and clear signposting all help. Ensure the content of worksheets is appropriate for the pupil's reading level.
- Highlight and explain subject-specific key words; display them around the room and provide a list for pupils to stick into their books/folders as a reference so that they become part of the pupils' sight vocabulary.
- Write clearly on the board, in large script; using different colours for alternate lines of writing can make it easier for students to follow.

43 Students with SLCD accessing the curriculum

Possible barriers	Strategies to try
Students struggle to read text books	• Find out the readability levels of texts used and compare with students' reading age (RA) • Have a range of texts available, including some with simple text, well-illustrated and 'sign-posted' with sub-headings, etc. • Read aloud from texts (avoid asking weak readers to do this without rehearsal) • Pair a confident reader with a weaker reader
Difficulties in following information/activity sheets/notes on the board	• Prepare simplified sheets/instructions • Use different colours on the board, for example, a different colour for each line to help students follow the text. In printed material, colour (of print and paper), font style and size, and space on the page can all make a difference to ease of reading
Does not easily absorb new vocabulary	• Highlight key words; explain them, look at the root, spelling and connected words, e.g. evaporate, evaporation, vapour • Provide lists of important words for a new topic to stick into books, and display on the wall; revisit and consolidate • Be aware of students' shaky understanding of 'academic' language; check that they really know what is meant by words such as 'define' 'analyse', 'discuss'
Doesn't read voluntarily: lack of practice slows progress	• Set reading for homework, asking students to share the key points in the next lesson • Recommend 'good reads' and encourage discussion about books

Possible barriers	Strategies to try

Finds it painfully difficult to write at any length in a coherent way	• Use directed activities related to text (DART):
	  ○ highlighting key words in text (photocopy sheets, or use acetate overlays)
	  ○ sequencing: provide, for example, the steps of a science investigation on strips of paper, where the student then has to read them and insert them into their book in the correct order
	  ○ cloze procedure: provide text with key words missing; the student writes in the appropriate words
	• Provide a writing frame, helping students to structure their writing
	• Deploy a skilled teaching assistant to help students plan and sequence their writing, perhaps formulating a mindmap as a starting point

Difficulties with the mechanics of writing	• Check that the pen is appropriate (something this simple can make a big difference) • Encourage the use of word processing, possibly with software such as Clicker 6 (www.cricksoft.com), which can speed up recording, help with vocabulary, spelling and sentence structure. Adjust computer screens and text size where appropriate; consider voice recognition software; predictive text; different types of spellcheckers
Poor spelling	• Use 'Look, say, cover, write, check' consistently • Encourage students to 'have a go' rather than always ask • Provide a range of dictionaries, including an ACE one (Aurally Coded English) • Provide word banks on tables/in student files

Takes a long time to produce writing	• Ensure that there are other ways of recording, for example:
	  ○ taking photos with a digital camera and adding text; using a video camera or making a recording using a computer and web cam
	  ○ verbal answers, presentations, role play
	  ○ making a storyboard or poster
	  ○ recording information in a table or as a spidergram
	• Encourage students to talk through what they are going to write – perhaps with a teaching assistant
	• Consider using role play to consolidate ideas
	• Provide a writing frame
	• Allow extra time for completion of written task – or adjust your expectations

Praise for effort as well as achievement – remember that students with weak literacy skills may have to work twice as hard to produce half as much as their peers

44 Supporting students with organisation

How can I find out? Where can I look for information?

- **Books**: in the classroom, school library, town library, at home (use the contents page and index to check quickly that the information is there).
- **People**: who can you ask? Teachers, other pupils, parents, family, neighbours. Could you make a telephone call, write a letter or send an email? Would it be useful to prepare **interview** questions or conduct a **survey**?
- **Film, DVD**: from school stock or the public library? Remember that films can be useful in providing background information but may not always be accurate with dates and specific facts – always double check.
- **The internet**: use a search machine or specific sites recommended by your teacher. Think carefully about which words you use in searching – and in which order, to get the best results. Remember that not all sites are reliable – as with films, you may need to double check.

How can I show what I've learned?

- Make **notes**: use titles, subtitles and bullet points; different colours for different issues. Always note down the title of the book you are using and if you use a quote, reference it correctly. (Who said/wrote it? When? Where?) These may later be redrafted into a more polished piece of writing.
- Make a **spidergram or mindmap**.
- Label **diagrams, drawings or photographs** to convey information and show understanding.
- Design a **poster or book cover**.
- Summarise information in a **table**.
- Produce a **role play or drama**.
- Make a **short film**.
- Make a **presentation** to other pupils.

45 Learning plans

High quality teaching is that which is differentiated and personalised to meet the needs of the majority of children and young people. Some children and young people need something additional to or different from what is provided for the majority of children; this is special educational provision and schools and colleges must use their best endeavours to ensure that provision is made for those who need it. Special educational provision is underpinned by high quality teaching and is compromised by anything less. (Code of Practice 2014)

Once a potential special educational need is identified, four types of action should be taken to put effective support in place. These actions form part of a cycle through which earlier decisions and actions are revisited, refined and revised with the growing understanding of the pupils' needs and of what supports the pupil in making good progress and securing good outcomes.

It is for schools and academies to determine their own approach to record keeping. But the Provision made for pupils with SEN should be accurately recorded and kept up to date. Ofsted will expect to see evidence of the support that is in place for pupils and the impact of that support on their progress. (C of P)

Teachers' Standards (Department of Education 2012)

Teaching

A teacher must:
- 'Set goals that stretch and challenge pupils of all backgrounds, abilities and dispositions…
- Adapt teaching to respond to the strengths and needs of all pupils
  - know when and how to differentiate appropriately, using approaches which enable pupils to be taught effectively…
  - have a clear understanding of the needs of all pupils, including: those with special educational needs; those of high ability; those with English as an additional language; those with disabilities; and be able to use and evaluate distinctive teaching approaches to engage and support them…
- Make accurate and productive use of assessment
  - know and understand how to assess the relevant subject and curriculum areas, including statutory requirements.'

What is on the Learning Plan is not the only matter for concern: it is how the plan is going to be implemented that is important.

© 2015, *Supporting Children with Speech and Learning Difficulties*
Allenby, Fearon-Wilson, Merrison and Morling, Routledge

Speech and language permeates the whole curriculum, indeed the whole school day. This means there are many opportunities to develop a child's speech and language.

Good planning can help to do this more effectively.

Useful starting points might be:

When is the best time to target specific language areas?
Who can best work with the child?

The following suggestions give examples of how to incorporate language targets into the curriculum.

Do remember:
It is important for the adult to secure the child's attention first and to give instructions in short, clear chunks.

Story in the English lesson (with the teacher)

Listening to and talking about a story can help develop:
- ✔ Attention control.
- ✔ Listening skills.
- ✔ Turn taking.
- ✔ Eye contact.
- ✔ Ability to respond appropriately to 'wh' questions.
- ✔ Reasoning skills, an understanding of cause and effect, empathy and the ability to infer and predict.

Group work in the English lesson (with the teacher or TA)

This does not need to be written work, but can be directed to the needs of the children involved.
- ✔ Circle time (see section on 'Circle Time').
- ✔ Specific language activities in small group.
- ✔ Link language and literacy targets (see section on 'Language in the National Literacy Strategy').

Around the classroom (teacher or TA)

- ✔ Giving instructions of increasing length will help develop the children's auditory memory skills, e.g. 'Put the ruler in the tray, your book in your drawer and line up at the door'.
- ✔ Giving instructions of increasing grammatical complexity will help develop the children's understanding of language, e.g 'Put the pencils on my desk and the books in the box under my desk'.

NB First make sure that the child understands simple concepts and can follow simple instructions.

> ### Individual session (with SEN teacher or TA)
>
> For some children, the most effective way to develop certain aspects of speech and language will be in individual sessions. Here, they can work on the targets provided by the speech and language therapist or SEN teacher. (See sample lesson plans.)

A comprehensive list of the way in which children's language can be developed across the curriculum areas can be found in *Teaching Talking* (Ann Locke & Maggie Beech: see 'Resources' section).

> ### Other curriculum areas (with class teacher/TA support)
>
> Language skills can be developed in all curriculum areas; this is effective because it means that language can be used more naturally and in context.
>
> It also means that a multi-sensory approach can be used and that objects and actions can be explored whilst language and concepts are developed.
>
> #### PE
>
> ✔ Memory and sequencing skills can be developed through a series of movements and actions.
> ✔ The children's knowledge of verbs can be developed, running, jumping, crawling etc.
> ✔ Parts of the body can be learnt, 'touch your knees', 'stand on one leg with your hands on your hips'.
> ✔ Specific concepts can be targeted, such as fast and slow, high and low etc.
> ✔ A knowledge of colours can be developed, 'run to a red ring', 'pick up a blue bean bag'.
>
> #### Science and Maths
>
> ✔ There are many concepts that can be worked on, for example: colours, hot and cold, light and heavy, more and less, longer and shorter.

46 Sample Learning Plans

The following are pen pictures of pupils with communication difficulties; one from a child from primary school and one from secondary school.

Tommy

Tommy is a little boy in Year 1. He is physically adept and always very cheerful. However, he finds it difficult to work on a task without having an adult with him to keep him focused. During Literacy he finds it hard to listen to a story without being distracted by what's going on around him. His responses to questions are often inappropriate. His answers tend to be short and his vocabulary non-specific, for example, he uses 'thingy' and 'there' a lot. When working in a group with his peers he has difficulty turn-taking and often interrupts other children.

Jenny

Jenny is a girl in Year 7 who has difficulty with social communication skills. She has problems with auditory memory, which results in her finding it hard to follow instructions. She does, however, have visual strengths, which means that she benefits from having visual prompts. At times she gives inappropriate responses to questions and finds it difficult to give explanations for choices or opinions.

> The provision made for pupils with SEN should be accurately recorded and kept up to date. Ofsted will expect to see evidence of the support that is in place for pupils and the impact of that support on their progress. (Code of Practice 2014)

The following are examples of methods of recording goals, activities and support that will help the pupil make progress. These may be determined by individual schools, academies and local authorities. They should be reviewed termly and the responsibility of the parent, pupil and school should also be identified.

Learning Plan

Name: Tommy .... DOB: .... NC Year: 1 .... Stage: ....

Teacher: .... Term: .... Date: .... Next Review Date: ....

Nature of difficulties:

	Targets	W	A	Strategies/Resources (including use of IT)	Evaluation
Attention	**Attention Control** Maintain attention to task with some intermittent support				
Receptive and Expressive Language Skills	Listen and respond to stories: Responds appropriately to questions about familiar or immediate events (who, what, where questions). Respond to questions about experiences, events and stories (who, what, where questions). Listen to, attend to and follow stories for short stretches of time.				
Interaction	**Participates in circle time:** Wait for turn to speak. Ask simple questions to obtain information. Communicate ideas about past, present and future events, using simple phrases.				

Learning Plan

Name: Jenny .... **DOB:** .... **NC Year:** 7 .... **Stage:** ....

Teacher: .... **Term:** .... **Date:** .... **Next Review Date:** ....

Nature of difficulties:

Targets	W	A	Strategies/Resources (including use of IT)	Evaluation
Listens to others in class, in group or in pairs, asks relevant questions and follows instructions. To be able to demonstrate effective use of visual strategies to support learning, for example, visual timetable, cue cards etc. Sustains conversation, explaining or giving reasons for views or choices.			Allow opportunity for pair and group work. Encourage interaction. To follow timetable with visual as well as written symbols to aid understanding, memory and sequencing skills. To allow Jenny to express herself without pressure, within class or group.	

47 Support staff: their effective use by teachers

Not all children with speech and language difficulties will require additional support in order to meet their needs within the classroom. For those pupils with a more significant level of need, however, the provision of support staff is vital to ensure that their needs can be met.

Teachers may wish to consider the following when deploying support staff:

- Support staff should promote independence in pupils with whom they are working.
- It may not be necessary to work alongside the pupil in every lesson.
- Allow the pupil to focus on the teacher, rather than on support staff.
- Support staff may need to take notes during teacher input for reference during a later part of the lesson.
- Liaison procedures between home and school should be established under the guidance of the SENCO, Head of Year or form teacher.
- Withdrawal of the pupil, in order to follow specific speech and language therapy programmes should be negotiated with the SENCO or teacher.

Teachers' Standards, 2012 state that teaching staff should 'Fulfil wider professional responsibilities' by 'Deploy[ing] support staff effectively'.

Code of Practice, 2014 states: 'Where the interventions involve group or one-to-one teaching away from the main class or subject teacher, they should still retain responsibility for the pupil, working closely with any teaching assistants or specialist staff involved, to plan and assess the impact of interventions'.

48 Support staff: initial and ongoing considerations

Support staff should:

Have a clear understanding of their roles and responsibilities:

- have a knowledge of their job description;
- maintain a professional demeanour with parents;
- be aware of school policies with regard to behaviour, anti-bullying, child protection;
- respect the confidentiality of information for all pupils.

Be aware of channels of communication within the school:

- ensure that information given by parents is given to the appropriate member of staff – class teacher, SENCO.
- ensure that communication with outside agencies is carried out in consultation with the SENCO.
- ensure that recommendations and reports from outside agencies are passed to the teacher and SENCO.
- ensure that information given to parents is with the knowledge of the class teacher.
- ensure that there is a mechanism for disseminating information to support staff about school activities, e.g. daily diary, staffroom notice board.

Be recognised as valued members of a team:

- participate in the planning and monitoring process.

Be encouraged to make use of their personal skills:

- share skills, e.g. ICT, creative skills.

Be supported with appropriate on-going professional development:

- observe and learn from other professionals in school and in other establishments.
- undertake training in school and through external courses.

Encourage the pupil's independence at all times:

- promote independent work habits.
- promote independent life skills.
- promote independent play skills.

49 Support staff: guidelines for working with pupils

Avoid	But instead...
sitting next to the pupil at all times	work with other pupils, while keeping an eye on the pupil you are assigned to
offering too close an oversight during breaks and lunchtimes	encourage playing with peers, introduce games to include others if necessary
collecting equipment for the pupil or putting it away	encourage the pupil to carry this out with independence
completing a task for a pupil	ensure that work is at an appropriate level and is carried out with minimal support (note any support given)
allowing behaviour which is not age-appropriate to the pupil, e.g. holding hands in the playground or in school	encourage the development of more age-appropriate peer relationships by social engineering, 'buddying' or circle of friends
making unnecessary allowances for the pupil	ensure that school rules apply
preventing the pupil from taking the consequences of their actions	insist that the pupil takes the responsibility for and the consequences of his/her actions
tolerating bad behaviour	follow the behaviour policy
making unrealistic demands on the pupil	ensure instructions and work are at the appropriate level
making decisions for the pupil	give the pupil opportunities to make choices and decisions
over-dependency on the support assistant	encourage independent behaviour and work

50 Working with parents

Parents are increasingly seen as partners with teachers in their child's education. This is particularly true in the area of speech and language, where parents have the opportunity to interact with their child and to develop their language.

Points for parents to remember:

- If you feel you need advice, ask your child's Speech and Language Therapist or teacher for support.
- You do not need to be following a structured programme to develop your child's language.
- Talk about everyday events like cleaning your teeth and washing the dishes.
- Talk about the things you can see on the way to school or playgroup.
- A good time to talk is when you are playing or making something together.
- Above all, make sure your time together is relaxed and enjoyable.

Points for teachers to remember:

- Remember to keep parents updated about their child's progress and to invite them to review meetings.
- Listen to their concerns and trust their knowledge of their child.
- Parents should be aware of the Code of Practice and what it means for their child.
- Encourage them to help in school, for example, with reading, cooking, etc.
- Use a home–school liaison book to talk about events; this will be particularly useful where a child's speech/language is difficult to understand.

51 Planning for continuing professional development (CPD)

With so many children entering school with speech, language and communication difficulties, it is more important than ever that all staff (including teaching assistants, lunchtime supervisors and support staff) feel able to meet their needs. The provision of carefully tailored continuing professional development (CPD) will help to build colleagues' confidence in this area and develop a consistent approach throughout the school.

An outline plan of CPD sessions might incorporate objectives such as ensuring that colleagues have:

- a sound knowledge of the issues involved (the difficulties encountered by children with SLCD, in different lessons, in the playground, outside school)
- the ability to identify children with SLCD
- the confidence to ask experienced colleagues for help and advice
- a range of strategies to meet individual needs and reduce barriers to learning

Format of CPD

The method of delivering professional development will depend on particular factors relating to the school as a whole, and to individual teachers and TAs. The opportunity to learn more about children with SLCD will be welcomed by colleagues who recognise children they teach, support or supervise as having difficulties – the issues are then immediately relevant. But it's also important for staff to appreciate that there may be pupils who experience difficulties but who have not been formally identified; for these children, basic good practice can make a significant difference to how well they can access learning.

There are many different formats of CPD to consider:

- **Whole-staff training during a CPD day, or staff meeting**. You may choose to invite an 'expert speaker', a colleague from a neighbouring school (perhaps a specialist school for SLCD), a member of your LA pupil support team or a speech and language therapist. If you do choose this option, be sure to brief the speaker adequately. He or she needs to know: the precise range and nature of SLCD in your school; what if any, interventions are in place; details of previous training received by staff.

  A school's SENCO is often the best person to plan and deliver such training as s/he knows the school, the staff and the children, and can ensure that information and advice offered is relevant and appropriate. Such a person can also build in opportunities for follow-up and ongoing development. Be 'in it together'; mutual vulnerability can be a powerful medium for exploring how changes to practice can result in positive developments.

- **Phase or pastoral group training**: scheduled sessions for TAs, EYFS staff, learning support team, etc. This may be focused on learning to use a specific approach or resource such as PECS (Picture Exchange Communication System), Makaton or Symbol Maker.
- **Sharing best practice** (sometimes referred to as 'joint practice development' – JPD): this is more about working together than about transferring knowledge or tips from one educator to another. Activities such as peer observation and shared planning can help to develop a sense of common purpose among staff.
- **Individual mentoring/coaching**: this can be particularly useful where a colleague is teaching a child with significant needs and has no previous experience of dealing with SLCD.
- **Individual study**: colleagues who strive to make good provision for SLCD pupils can become very interested in finding out more, even developing expertise in the field. Pursuing a course of study at university, attending a PECS course or locally provided training should be encouraged and supported – with the proviso that there will be some form of dissemination to colleagues. This course of action can be particularly beneficial to TAs tasked with delivering intervention programmes and/or supporting individual children with SLCD.
- **Encourage professional reading** in small groups or individually. Place new relevant books (including this one!) in the staffroom library; seek out and share articles and research studies as food for thought, as well as reviews of useful resources. Perhaps devote five minutes of meeting time to highlight why you have selected particular reading matter. Encourage staff to contribute to this process too. Perhaps use social networking or your school's virtual learning environment to facilitate it.

52 An outline for whole-school training on SLCD

1. Explain the range of speech, language and communication difficulties (expressive, receptive, etc.) and additional factors such as attention span, social skills and sometimes, general developmental delay (see page 1). You might actively involve colleagues in this by giving out a 'sorting activity' of all the various ways that SLCD can manifest. (Use the grid on page 83 and perhaps ask colleagues to prioritise those factors that are the most challenging to identify and/or deal with; or ask them which behaviours they have observed in children they teach.)

2. Ask colleagues if they have ever been in a situation where they could not make themselves understood (perhaps because of a language barrier). How did they feel? If time allows, it can be useful to task them with explaining something to a partner, without speaking or writing – give out examples such as 'I would like to have pasta for my lunch'; 'I need to go to the toilet'; 'I'm feeing very unhappy'. Can they suggest how children with communication difficulties can be helped to express themselves effectively?

3. Identifying children with SLCD. What should colleagues be looking out for? What is the school system for referral? (Use/amend the chart on page 5.)

4. Classroom strategies: use the strategies listed throughout this book to put together a good practice guide.

5. Effective use of TAs: see the guidance on page 76.

6. Interventions: make sure that staff are familiar with what happens during any specialist sessions. Can colleagues observe an intervention group in action? How can they support and reinforce this work?

7. Parents: how can colleagues garner parents' support and help them to help their children? (See page 79.)

53 What does SLCD mean for a child?

Limited attention – easily distracted
Seems to ignore/fails to follow instructions
Difficulty in identifying different sounds (weak auditory discrimination), learning phonics
Does not understand complex instructions or questions
Anxiety
Does not understand 'yesterday, today, tomorrow, next week/year'
Becomes confused and disorientated in the bustle of school life
Limited vocabulary and word-finding difficulties – may resort to 'the thingy'
Child's speech is difficult to understand – 'assembly' difficulties (e.g. 'par cark'); may not be understood
Frustration and low self-esteem
Poor spelling
May read accurately but with limited understanding of text
Difficulties in making and keeping friends
Struggles to follow class discussion and unable to answer questions
Finds turn-taking difficult
May have difficulties with prediction, sequencing and inference
Unable to express difficulties and ask for help
May not understand jokes, word-play and figurative language, e.g. 'keep your hair on'

54 Evaluating and following up CPD

Whichever mode of CPD is delivered (you may chose a mixed menu), it's important to evaluate its effectiveness and plan for ongoing development. Consider a short evaluation sheet for staff to complete after a training session on SLCD, including their suggestions and requests for further development opportunities.

Taking this information into consideration, you can then plan follow-up work to consolidate and build on the training delivered. This provides good accountability evidence for senior managers and OFSTED, and demonstrates the school's (and SENCO's) effectiveness. Ideas for follow-up activities are suggested below.

- A regular 'surgery' where teachers and TAs can seek advice from the SENCO or speech and language therapist
- Optional 'advanced' CPD for interested staff
- Opportunities for teachers to observe intervention programmes – in your own school or elsewhere
- A working party to trial a new approach or piece of new technology
- An action-research project to test an intervention and report back to staff on its effectiveness
- Classroom observations by the SENCO to monitor colleagues' effectiveness in providing for the needs of children with SLCD
- Detailed tracking of children with SLCD to monitor progress and evaluate strategies being used to support them

Glossary

Articulators
Parts of the vocal apparatus, such as the palate, tongue or voice box.

Attention Control
The ability to focus on stimuli when requested or required, for example, being able to listen to teacher's instructions while writing.

Auditory Discrimination
The ability to notice differences in sounds within words, for example, 'bat' and 'pat', 'kin' and 'king'.

Auditory Short-term Memory
The ability to hold and process information within the working memory resulting in being able, for example, to carry out instructions or blend sounds into a word.

Dysfluency
Inability to control fluency of speech production, resulting in hesitancy, stuttering, etc.

Expressive Language
Using spoken language to communicate.

Grammar/syntax
The rules by which words are combined to produce sentences.

Intonation
Variations in pitch when talking, which may change word meaning.

Morpheme
The smallest unit of meaning which may be a word (as in 'hat' or 'jump') or a word ending; for example, the plural 's' in 'hats', the 'ed' in 'jumped'.

Non-verbal Skills
The ability to communicate without using words, for example, body language, eye contact or gesture.

Phonics
The relationship between speech sounds and letters.

Phonological Awareness
The ability to hear and reflect upon sounds within words, for example an appreciation of rhyme and syllables.

Phonology
The separate sounds within words and the rules that govern the way they occur.

Pragmatics
The aspect of meaning concerned with what someone says and the context in which they say it.

Processing
Understanding what is said and organising what you want to say.

Prosody
The use of intonation, rhythm, speed and volume in language.

Receptive Language
Understanding or comprehension of spoken language.

Semantics
The meanings of words.

Resources

Assessment and intervention

Afasic   www.afasic.org.uk
Language Checklists: Speech and language screening tests for children aged 4–5 and 6–10
Indicators Checklist (for non-specialist staff)
Is Your School a Communication Friendly School?
Listening to Children and Young People with Speech, Language and Communication Needs

Early Language Skill Checklist   James Boyle and Elizabeth McLellan
                                       Hodder & Stoughton, 1998
(An observation based checklist for children aged 3–5 with language difficulties)

GAPS Test   www.dldcn.com
(A grammar and phonology screening test to identify language impaired children)

Time to Talk: Implementing Outstanding Practice in Speech, Language and Communication   Jean Gross
                                       Routledge, 2013
                                       www.routledge.com

Activities and games

Activities for Speaking and Listening   AFASIC
Part 1: Ages 3 to 7   www.afasic.org.uk
Part 2: Ages 7 to 11

Working with Children's Language   Jackie Cooke and Diane Williams
                                       www.speechmark.net

Language GAP   Sue Gowers and Libby Sisson
                                       Senter, 1995
(A language programme, which looks at auditory memory, categorisation, verbal absurdities etc.)

CLEAR Pictoys Sets 1–10   www.clear-resources.co.uk
(A set of games designed to build understanding and use of language from one-to four-word level)

Language Steps   Amanda Armstrong
                                            www.winslowresources.com
(Designed to develop understanding and use of language from one- to four-word level)

Stories for Talking   Rebecca Bergmann
                                            www.qed.uk.com

Black Sheep resources   www.blacksheeppress.co.uk

LDA publications   www.ldalearning.com

Winslow resources and publications   www.winslowresources.com

Phonology

Working with Children's Phonology   Gwen Lancaster and Lesley Pope
                                            Winslow Press, 1997

Children's Phonology Sourcebook   Lesley Flynn and Gwen Lancaster
                                            Winslow Press, 1997

Phonology Barrier Game   Black Sheep Press
                                            www.blacksheeppress.co.uk

Caroline Bowen   www.speech-language-therapy.com
(Online information and resources)

Social communication

Semantic-Pragmatic Language Disorder   Charlotte Firth and Katherine Venkatesh
                                            Winslow Press, 1999

Social Skills Stories   Anne Marie Johnson and Jackie L. Susnik
                                            www.mayer-johnson.com

Social Use of Language Programme (SULP)
                                            Wendy Rinaldi
                                            www.wendyrinaldi.com

Talkabout: A Social Communication Skills Package Alex Kelly
                                            www.speechmark.net

Don't Take it So Literally: Reproducable Activities for Teaching Idioms
                                            Danielle M. Legler
                                            ECL Publications, 1991

Explore Social Skills   Don Johnston
                                            www.donjohnston.com
(An intervention programme for adolescents and young adults)

Circle Time: A Practical Book of Circle Time Lesson Plans
Jenny Mosley
Positive Press, 2001
www.circle-time.co.uk

101 Games for Social Skills   Jenny Mosely and Helen Sonnet
www.circle-time.co.uk

Visual cues

The Picture Exchange Communication System (PECS)
www.pecs-unitedkingdom.com

Picture Communication Symbols (PCS)   Mayer-Johnson
www.mayer-johnson.com

Software

Apps for tablets and iPads   www.inclusive.co.uk
www.appolearning.com
www.myfirstapp.com
www.alligatorapps.com
www.tribalnova.com
www.innivo.com
www.mayer-johnson.com/apps (PCS)
www.remarkableapps.com

Boardmaker   www.mayer-johnson.com

Communication in Print   www.widgit.com

Clicker   www.cricksoft.com

Picure Sentence Key   software.informer.com

Resource websites

Black Sheep Press   www.blacksheeppress.co.uk

Caroline Bowen   www.speech-language-therapy.com

CLEAR Resources   www.clear-resources.co.uk

LDA   www.ldalearning.com

Speechmark   www.speechmark.net

STASS   www.stasspublications.co.uk

Taskmaster   www.taskmasteronline.co.uk

Winslow   www.winslowresources.com

Good listening rules

✓ good looking

✓ good sitting

✓ good thinking

Lightning Source UK Ltd.
Milton Keynes UK
UKHW031426051119
352907UK00013B/94/P